WHEN I WAS YOUNG

VOICES *from* LOST COMMUNITIES *in* SCOTLAND: *The* ISLANDS

TIMOTHY NEAT

BIRLINN LIMITED

THIS BOOK IS DEDICATED TO FRANCIS AND FRANCESCA MARUBINI NEAT
MARRIED AT GRESSONEY ST JEAN, 29th MAY 1999

First published in 2000 by
Birlinn Limited
8 Canongate Venture
5 New Street
Edinburgh
EH8 8BH

Previous page.
Donald Ferguson with Joujou on the
North French coast, 1925. (JFM)

ISBN 1 84158 039 2

British Library Cataloguing-in-Publication Data
A catalogue record for this book is available from the British Library

Text and layout design by Mark Blackadder

The publisher acknowledges subsidy from

THE SCOTTISH ARTS COUNCIL

towards the publication of this book

Printed and bound by The Bath Press, Glasgow

Contents

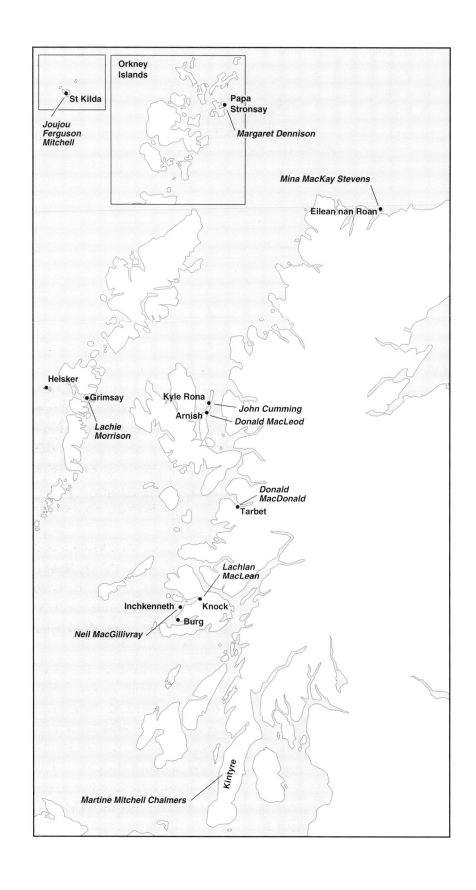

Orkney Islands

St Kilda

Joujou Ferguson Mitchell

Papa Stronsay

Margaret Dennison

Mina MacKay Stevens

Eilean nan Roan

Heisker

Grimsay

Lachie Morrison

Kyle Rona

John Cumming

Arnish

Donald MacLeod

Donald MacDonald

Tarbet

Lachlan MacLean

Inchkenneth

Knock

Burg

Neil MacGillivray

Kintyre

Martine Mitchell Chalmers

Preface

When I Was Young is a book that grew and changed in the writing. It was planned as one volume. It has become two. The plan was to document the lives of people from 'lost communities' in the Highlands of Scotland, but there are so many such communities and so many people with direct memories of them that it seemed a betrayal to have the boundaries of such a subject defined by the width of a paperback binding. Thus, with the encouragement of my publisher, Hugh Andrew, the book expanded into two volumes. Now, although they explore a huge subject via an apparently arbitrary selection of individuals, they are wide-ranging; they have depth and are broadly representative.

   The two volumes have been divided geographically. The first deals with lives lived in the Hebrides, on Eilean nan Roan and the Orkney island of Stronsay (and touches Paris and Australia). The second presents life in the Highlands and along Scotland's eastern seaboard, north of the Tay (and the Arctic seaboard of Canada). As in all my books, photography and poetry play a crucial part in both the documentation and the narrative development.

   These two new volumes are books three and four of what will become a 'Highland Quintet'. The aim has been to create a contemporary, literary record of traditional life in the Highlands and Islands by means of biographical portraiture. The first book, *The Summer Walkers*, published in 1996, documented the lives and lifestyle of travelling people and pearl-fishers. The second, *The Voice of the Bard*, published in 1999, explored the lives of poets continuing the Gaidhealtachtd's ancient bardic tradition in the twentieth century. The last volume, *The Horseman's Word*, will present the lives, the work and beliefs of blacksmiths, farriers and horsemen. Each book gives the page to selected individuals from selected communities or occupational groups, but the five volumes together will, I believe, create a surprisingly complete 'group self-portrait' of Highland Life in the twentieth century.

————————————

'When I was young' is a phrase frequently used by older people, not just in Scotland but everywhere, and across the world the ruins of 'lost communities' are to be found in vast numbers – uninhabited homesteads; roofless villages; scarred headlands and crumbling quays; deserted islands; vacated hill forts; bare mountainsides which once were walled and farmed. Nowhere is the loss of such communities felt more keenly than in Scotland, where memory and history are deeply part of life. Memory, the early Greeks believed, was Mother of the Muses. And so in Scotland to this day. In particular, memory – 'thought recollected in tranquility' – infuses the poetry and song of Scotland, and these twin art-forms have played a major part in the lives – the inspiration, the sense of 'lived history' – to which these books and this Quintet play tribute:

> It's early morning, as I rise in high spirits,
> It's early morning in springtime and I am in Os:
> The cattle are lowing as they mingle together
> And the sun rising on the flat heights of the Storr,
> Light, unfolding the thighs of the mountain,
> Vanquishing night as dark melts into day;
> And above me the lark is joyous in song
> – Lifting my thoughts to when I was young.

> It brings to my mind many things that I did,
> Things intertwined in my soul, whilst I live,
> Going in winter to waulkings and weddings,
> No lantern to hand but the blaze-end of a peat
> And joyful the young at their music and dancing:
> But now, looking back, I see the glen in dark sorrow,
> The house of Andrew is brimming with nettles,
> – Lifting my thoughts to when I was young.

Those verses, translated from the song 'Nuair bha mi Og', give these volumes their title. It was composed by the renowned nineteenth-century Skye bard 'Big Mary of the Songs' (Mairi Mhor nan Oran), and it gives classic expression to one of the deep and permanent sensibilities of the Gael – the comprehension of beauty, of nature, of history as loss as every generation experiences the Genesis story afresh. And many of Mairi Mhor's various, courageous and heroic qualities will be found in the lives and characters presented in these pages – continuity has been of the essence in the Highlands. Such conservatism can lead to ossification, but genuine continuity demands rigour and choices and it would be wrong to assume the stories revealed in these volumes are further examples of the sentimental nostalgia that has bedevilled too much Highland reportage. These biographies are grounded in facts, in realities and are continuously surprising.

      After a century of decline, the population of many parts of Northern Scotland is once more on the increase. Comparatively good roads, the car, aeroplanes, television, computers and the Internet have concertinaed distance. Electricity, waterproofs, central heating, mechanical appliances and subsidies of various kinds have brought increased comfort and leisure. Tourism, oil, new ideas and a new political and cultural confidence have cemented change and a new vitality across the whole of the Highlands and Islands. Much has been improved, but things have also been lost, including whole communities – communities of the kinds profiled, via individual memory, in these pages.

      Memory is a peculiar and powerful force. To a considerable extent all human memories are 'constructed'. In assembling memories, one of the first tasks of the mind is to forget, and it often takes time for this to happen. Memory needs time to assume form and this is done by both conscious and unconscious siftings of what each individual believes to have been the wheat and chaff of their experience. It takes time for the mind to pan the gold from sand. This process is subject to psychological and creative manipulation – external as well as internal – and in this process of assemblage everyone, to some extent, becomes an artist. We choose and frame our memories (just as we choose our ancestries and historical allegiance) and all memories share the strengths and weaknesses of all private preserves. The remembrancer, like the artist, continually re-conceives, reshapes and reviews his subject until it assumes a permanence, a beauty, a certain grandeur or horror – a rightness. Only then does it lock in the memory and become long-term 'reconstructed truth'. And rather as it is necessary for the painter to have his work seen and recognised; as it is necessary for the musician to have his work heard and enjoyed; as it is necessary for the poet to have his words read and thought about – so each one of us collates memories and would like them to be recognised. The archetypal example of this is T.S. Coleridge's Ancient Mariner accosting passers-by on the quays of Watchet harbour.

      The art of memory is one of the great, hidden cultural forces in society and there can be no doubt that these books, whilst they are on one level documentation, are also culturally determined: first by my own wish to give the books, as books, significant and permanent form; and second by the measured nature of the much patinaed memories relayed by the informants and subjects.

These volumes are therefore, at once, both documents and poetic constructs. My colleague, the poet and folklorist, Hamish Henderson, has a wonderful phrase, 'Poetry becomes people'. No vital poetry can turn its back on people, nor a society flourish without some openness to poetic forces. Poetry reveals, nurtures, elevates and affirms. That is what these books set out to do.

The transience of human life is a fact understood by children at a remarkably early age, yet they, like adults, also have a strange longing to see both the past and the future as stable entities linked to their own existence, and they comprehend 'continuity' as a given. 'Live every day as though it were your last but farm as though you would live for ever' is a phrase used more by farmworkers than by farmers, but it speaks for us all. People everywhere assume the Earth to be permanent, and most feel strong physical, genealogical and spiritual bonds between themselves and their place of abode, especially if it is ancestral ground. This is particularly true of traditional communities living in rural environments or amidst archetypal nature. Such local dominion can nurture the hunger for external adventure, but more often it validates the deep human instinct to belong, both to a place and to a community. It is this instinct, combined with social, religious and cultural forms, that have ensured that clearly defined peoples (the Jews, the Scots, the Italians are clear examples) can carry their identifiable selves, as individuals and as cohesive social groups, for many generations after permanent geographical displacements occurred.

At the beginning of the twenty-first century, rapid economic change is pushing still increasing numbers of people from rural to urbanised environments. Youth, in particular, is drawn abroad by the magnetic appeal of education, work, money, sex and westernised culture – the heady dream of individual freedom and personal fulfilment. If the huge expansion of the world's population continues, it is unlikely that the future will witness the widespread, total loss of communities that has been common over the last three centuries, because sheer weight of numbers and increased human mobility will ensure that most habitable places remain inhabited. But the pace of demographic and social change does necessitate the need for an awareness of the importance of remembrance and social conservation. On a treadmill of material well-being and urbanity, we should not forget the values and best habits nurtured across millenia – social, convivial, moral, enduring. We cannot resurrect truly 'lost communities', but we can recognise and honour the qualities they had (think how many worse things are encouraged, studied and subsidised all around us). As much as birds, mammals, habitats, moorland and mountain, isolated communities deserve our recognition and support, if only in retrospect.

Modern European man is about 30,000 years old. That is a short span of time in life's evolutionary chain. Recent biological studies of the human species have rightly emphasised our animal evolution over millions of years, but, squeezed between immemorial genetic heredity and exponential technological advance, we should not forget the importance of the socio-cultural accretions of those fifteen hundred human generations since our Cro-Magnon forebears gained dominance over our Neanderthal 'uncles'. And in estimating the value of the past we should note that whereas many of the physical products of man's best-being are well cared for in the world's libraries, art galleries, museums and great houses, many of our purely human treasures lie exposed, vulnerable and often decried. Prime amongst these are the ways of life and the collective wisdom of the world's still extant, much put upon traditional communities. Money speaks and such communities are almost by definition poor, but, for millennia, they have husbanded values the galloping, technological world would be foolish to forget. The long-term consequences of uncontrolled growth are at least as insidious as decay and atrophy:

> I remember the late Conan Doyle remarking
> How a glorious cancer, like marble compares,
> To the miserable carrion it batons upon –

There is profound truth in that brilliant image, created by Hugh MacDiarmid in a poem about the overweening conceit of the University of Edinburgh. And it maybe that, in the long term, the growth, vigour and beauty of Western materialism will prove to have been not the life-giving dynamism of youth but a malignant cancer in the throat of the world.

And tradition should be recognised as having crucially underpinned most of the great surges human civilisations have made. The rational classicism and love of proportion in Ancient Greece was enormously dependent on the fantastic Mediterranean heritage that preceded it. The centuries old pre-eminence of the bourgeois culture of France is still founded on the labour, the sensuality, the pride of her artisans and peasantry. How deeply the knowledge-revolution of the Italian renaissance depended on exquisite medieval craftsmanship. How much the world's 'great' music has grown tall on the 'uncomposed' riches of the various folk traditions. How much Shakespeare, Joyce and Burns depended on the colloquial speech of their fellows in the taverns, the woods and the fields. How precisely the world's post-war freedoms depended on Serb, Russian and Highland valour. And how easy it is to forget. Isolation, poverty and phlegmatic hardihood have provided the armature on which many of the world's great achievements rest: the origin of the word 'civilisation' is the Greek word that means 'to lie down, or be recumbent', and through all history no peoples have been free to be recumbent and think of

higher, better things, but by the labour and sacrifice of others – with their hands
to plough, the net and the wheel.

>A bonnet on two sticks
>Is tomb for the Gael;
>Callum Mhor, mak
>Mane for Argyll. (HH)

Hardship and the lack of material possessions frequently enhances the wish for
belonging, and there can be few peoples in the world who identify themselves
more strongly with their native place than the Scots. 'We are born in the
Mountains and when we hire ourselves out to the Princes of the Lowlands,
sooner or later we feel an incurable homesickness. Because we are made for a
Higher Place we are gnawed by an Incurable Longing for the music of the
cowbells that remind us of home. There is a second world inside us that demands
a second world outside us …'

Those very Scottish sentiments were written in the eighteenth
century by the German Romantic Jean Paul Richter and they prove the
universality of human spirituality and love, but just as there are certain kinds of
mountainous landscape that are particularly spiritually evocative, so there are
certain built forms of universal beauty – notably those which evolved in Classical
Greece. For example the Scots artist Ian Hamilton Finlay has recently made a
series of works exploring cultural continuity around the theme of his own
evocative sentence, 'For the temples of the Greeks our homesickness lasts
forever.' Now architecture is not a high card in the pack of Gaelic achievements
but music, poetry and memory undoubtedly are, and there is a real sense in
which the Gaelic historical experience provides the world with one of the great
archetypes of human cultural experience – its music, in particular, speaking
directly and belonging to us all.

Everywhere, mountains and the sea nurture social cohesion,
character and spiritual belief. In Scotland, over the last 2000 years, an ancient
oral culture has very naturally allied itself with the imported written 'Word' of
the Hebrew God and the Testaments of Christ's disciples. In both traditions, the
Word – sung, spoken, written, illumined and studied – has been of pre-eminent
importance, and there is every reason not to be surprised that the people these
books represent speak so well and sing so often.

All the people profiled here have been strongly influenced by the
landscapes and environments in which they have lived, but it is equally true that
the human imagination can affect powerfully the ways in which landscape and
environments are perceived. Familiarity will sometimes blunt apprehension, but

familiarity can also awaken and fill in perception. Those who feel more see more and search more enquiringly. Coleridge believed that all good biographical writing depended on the way in which writers blend external and internal factors and makes them particular in living portraiture. What ignites the attention of the reader of any biography, he wrote, is the feeling that they are on 'a pilgrimage to see a great man's shin found unmouldered in a coffin'.

These two volumes collate short biographies of two dozen people brought up amidst grand natural environments, most of whom are still living. The stories they tell are rarely bizarre and never salacious but they do reveal vivid realities – and the photographs play a crucial role in these revelations. All photographs document moments in time and the transient nature of the medium seems to imbue photographic images with a rare poignancy. Photographs, like lives, are fugitive and transitory. The sense of intimacy that photography nurtures is used deliberately here, like the first person narrative, to give the books immediacy and the characters portrayed palpable reality.

One striking theme which recurs throughout the 'Highland Quintet' is that of superstition. Isolation and danger have always nurtured superstition in peoples vulnerable to events and powers beyond their control. Such vulnerability is a fact of Highland life and the common lot of soldiers, sailors, fishermen, small farmers, lovers, gamblers. Heroism, fateful stoicism – codified as superstitious belief – is one way of dealing with exposed circumstances and, like memory, superstition can be seen as an attempt by the mind, and whole communities, to deal with the uncontrollable and the catastrophic by creative, divergent thinking. Superstition, like surrealism, can give order, drama, meaning, variety and fantastic release to lives lived at the edge of experience. It can give excitement to minds deprived of serious, interactive intellectual and imaginative enquiry. The 'second sight' and the 'third eye' can also be recognised as bastardised art forms – folk-art remnants of shamanistic tradition and the continuing impulse.

And when I am in the boards
My words will be as prophesy,

And there will return the stock of the tenantry
Who were driven over the sea.

And the 'beggars' of gentry
Will be routed as the crofters were;

Deer and sheep will be wheeled away
And the glen will be tilled.

A time of sowing and reaping
And a time of come-uppance for robbers;

And the cold ruined stances of houses
Will be built-up by our kinsmen.

In that prophetic song, 'Faistnechd agus Beannachd do na Gaidheil', Mairi Mhor nan Oran brings the vision with which this preface begins full-circle. The idyll of a lost past here becomes an idyll of the future happiness of the Highland people. Both songs imagine landscapes conjured by the mind but both are also stoutly based in realities and possibilities – like the lives and stories relayed in these pages.

Everyone featured in these books is directly associated with a community which exists no longer or has utterly changed. Each is a remarkable character with vivid recall of a vanished, or disappearing, way of life. Yet the difference between these 'voices' and the 'ordinary voices' we hear every day in the street, in the home, on television, is small. The compelling power of these recollections is largely a matter of degree – most people accumulate extraordinary experience through their lives … But degrees add up and small gaps can become gulfs. What is it that divides great and timeless works of art from the mass of artistic production? Coleridge explored ideas of this kind as he sailed, beneath a full moon, through the Straits of Gibraltar: 'This is Africa! This is Europe! There is division, sharp boundary, abrupt change! But what are they in Nature? Two mountain banks that make a noble river of the interfluent sea – no division, no change, no antithesis …' Everything depends on who you are, what you think, what you feel, what you see, where you stand and what stands around you, where you come from, where you will go. And there *is* a difference between the lives of half a dozen children brought up on Eilean nan Roan off the Sutherland coast amidst Presbyterian rigour and the lives of thousands of children being brought up in Shakespeare's now suburban, multicultural West Midlands. Both experiences are vivid but one is relatively common, the other very rare. These books are proud to present that which was always rare, and will not be again.

The reasons for the collapse of the communities profiled here are many and varied, but one common thread would appear to be the unwillingness of even the most stoical and historically-aware communities to continue an existence based upon endless physical hardship when the opportunity of an easier livelihood elsewhere is there to be taken. In our monied, open, free and international society, it is apparent that not more than two or three generations will tolerate subservience to the endless demands of a subsistence economy. In extremis, families, groups, whole societies will dig-in and suffer, short-term, for the benefits of what they believe will be a better future. This is well documented in the Highlands and Islands, and in the Soviet Union, where tens of millions of people suffered terrible personal hardship in the hope (or under the delusion) that their present suffering would lead to the future well-being, not just of their families, but of all mankind. But, when a third generation sees its much-vaunted 'goal' fading ever further into the distance, the demand for change becomes overwhelming. Of course, Scotland and Britain might have supported our isolated Highland kinsmen with greater commitment than they did, and the Western World might have sought to build-up, not destroy, Soviet society. But it is also certain that relentless physical, social and biological forces beyond normal political bounds were at work in both cases.

Another factor in the loss of numerous small Highland communities was loss of a certain 'critical mass'. Anthropological studies suggest that the key natural size for the human group is that of the extended family, or tribal group, and consists of about 150 people (the traditional size of a British army regiment). Smaller groups can survive, but a stable number of active workers is necessary where self-sufficiency is normal and where boats or other large objects need to be man-handled. Once a population falls below a particular number the whole community can become non-viable very quickly. The re-routing of a road, a bout of disease, the condemnation of a house, the loss of a boat can turn a vulnerable subsistence community into an unsustainable relic. The noble tradition of shared labour can also quickly become a source of resentment – too much is required of too few and the shared burden becomes, of necessity, unfair.

Lack of numbers in isolated communities also raises sexual questions. Many youngsters feel compelled to move away, and even the most willing of incomers can find acceptance into closed communities very difficult. The education of the young and the care of the old – processes that naturally bind communities – can also, quite suddenly, become physical impossibilities that lead to communal dissolution. In Scotland the discipline of firm religious belief seems to have held some groups together for, perhaps, two generations longer than circumstances would have normally dictated, but even the proudest and most stoical communities will not continue to endure unremitting hardship for more than about a hundred years when alternatives exist.

If asked, however, to select the single most direct cause of the collapse of the communities profiled, I should choose the First World War. It came at a historical moment when its human and social impact was to prove devastating, not just in terms of the numbers of men killed, but of the many-sided

economic and cultural consequences it set in train. The great Highland virtues
became liabilities abroad: heroic martial tradition aggravated the scale of military
losses (in actions in which technology more than valour frequently shaped ends),
and, at home, the ideal of service drained a whole generation away in a new,
essentially voluntary 'Clearance' which saw thousands upon thousands leaving the
scattered communities of north Scotland – as nurses, nannies, governesses,
teachers, doctors, engineers, labourers, emigrants – never to return. The world
was enriched, but traditional patterns of fertility were hugely affected, and,
amongst those who remained, Highland 'propriety' too often outshone biological
need. So many bachelors, even more spinsters, and so few illigitimate children.
The population plummeted between 1910 and 1950. Money, for the first time,
had become an absolutely crucial adjunct to even the soundest subsistence
economies, and during the first half of the twentieth century, hard cash became
extremely difficult to earn in all parts of rural Scotland. But, for all that, the
scene can be painted too bleak – great things are always done when men and
women and mountains meet, and it is from scenes like these that old Scotia's
grandeur sprang and springs:

> O Scotia! My dear, my native soil
>   That makes her loved at home, revered abroad:
> Long may thy hardy sons of rustic toil,
>   Be blest with health, and peace, and sweet content!
> And, O! May Heav'n their simple lives prevent
>   From luxury's contagion, weak and vile:
> Then, howe'er crowns and coronets be rent,
>   A virtuous populous may rise the while,
> And stand a wall of fire around the much-loved isle.

Burns' poem 'The Cottar's Saturday Night' finishes with a rhetorical flourish but,
as a whole, paints a picture recognisably still part of traditional life in Scotland
and, for all his overbrimming individualism and genius, Burns accommodated the
rigours of circumstance, Kirk and State, just as the citizens portrayed here have
done. *When I was Young* is not a lament but a celebration of endurance and joy. For
is not Tir nan Og, 'The Land of the Always Young', always, naturally, with us?

The story of St Kilda is the classic story of a lost community in Scotland, and the
world. For that very reason I was going to exclude it from this book, but, for more
than twenty-five years, I have known two exceptional women descended from one
of the great men of St Kilda, Donald Ferguson, and, in the end, I felt impelled to

tell their marvellous stories. Joujou Mitchell and Martine Chalmers have lived happy and successful lives in Paris, Glasgow, Kintyre and the Auvergne – yet St Kilda remains the fulcrum of their sense of belonging. Their commitment to romantic love and spiritual truth and their social consciences add something special to the world's knowledge of the St Kildan people, as do the magnificent, largely unpublished photographs taken by Joujou's husband, Eddie Roslyn Mitchell.

Not all participants in this project are old friends. I only met Donald MacLeod of Arnish on the island of Raasay for three days – glorious June days – in 1998. And I met him by chance, striding through the birch woods at Eyre. But in three days we struck up a marvellous close friendship. Donald MacLeod is a shy, silent man, but he knows the crofting life of Raasay and embodies much of Highland tradition. As his distant relative, Sorley MacLean, wrote:

> And be what was as it was,
> I am of the big men of Braes,
> The heroic Raasay MacLeods,
> Of the sharp-sword Mathesons of Lochalsh;
> And the men of my name – who were braver
> When their ruinous pride was kindled?

Lachie Morrison of Grimsay, North Uist, is a remarkable man from a family of poets and singers, and as the new century dawns, the story of his life stands as a symbol of hope and renewal in the Hebrides. His father's attempt to recolonise the abandoned island of Heisker ended in failure, but now, in his seventies, Lachie is raising a young Gaelic-speaking son named after his father, whilst his wife, Theona, runs a new weaving business, selling the dark soft wool of the rare Hebridean sheep to fashion-houses round the world.

Mina MacKay Stevens of John O' Groats is one of the last survivors of Eilean nan Roan, a unique community which lived for generations – frequently marooned – off the north coast of Sutherland. At the age of eighty-eight, her memory is vivid, poetic and precise, and she provides telling insights into how life was lived and how things were for the girls and the women.

It was through my daughter, Mary Acheson, a teacher at Stronsay School, that I got to know Margaret Dennison and the small Orkney island of Papa Stronsay. Margaret's people were farmers who came down from Fair Isle. Papa Stronsay is an islet off a small island in the Orkney archipelago. It carries thousands of years of history and it encapsulates, in miniature, the extraordinary story of the rise and fall of Scotland's herring industry.

Neil MacGillivray and Lachie MacLean live within ten miles of each other on the island Mull but they have very different stories to tell. Knowledge of history is important to both men. Lachie is, in his own unassuming way, a *shennachie*, a remembrancer, amongst his people; Neil, a man who ferried Hitler's mistress many times across that short spread of water between Mull and Inchkenneth. How much they both have that the world is the better for knowing. And that is also true of Donald MacDonald of Tarbet, Loch Fyne, a man of Highland pride and Catholic humility. He has lived a life of almost monastic solitude and quietness. He was a postman, and as such stands as a symbol of another crucial figure in Highland life.

John Ruskin, the nineteenth-century art critic, described 'the most solemn virtue of Scotland' as 'the domestic truth and tenderness breathed in all Scottish song', and I hope readers will feel a continuing breath of that tradition in the stories and photographs presented here. And because the photographs are so important, I finish with a poem by the great twentieth-century art critic, John Berger – a man whom Lachie MacLean, Joujou Mitchell and Martine Chalmers know well:

When I open my wallet
to show my papers,
pay money
or check the time of a train,
I look at your face.

The flower's pollen
is older than the mountains,
Avaris is young
as mountains go,

The flower's ovules
will be seeding still
when Avaris, then aged,
is no more than a hill.

The flower in the heart's
wallet, the force
of what lives us,
outliving the mountain.

And our faces, my heart, brief as photos.

ACKNOWLEDGEMENTS

Many people in many communities across many generations have contributed to the making of this book. I thank them deeply. In particular Donald MacLeod of Arnish; Calum the Road; John Cumming and Calum MacKay of Raasay; Sorley and Rene MacLean; Lachie and Theona Morrison; Mina MacKay Stevens; Babsie MacKay of Thurso; Dave Illingworth and the Skerray Heritage Centre; Donald MacDonald of Tarbet; Margaret Dennison of Stronsay; Neil MacGillivray of the Aird of Kinloch; Lachie MacLean of Knock; Joujou Ferguson Mitchell and Martine Mitchell Chalmers. Also Iain Fraser of Dingwall; the photographer Peter Adamson; Will and Marion MacLean; Hamish Henderson of Glen Shee; John Berger of Quincey; Ian Hamilton Finlay of Little Sparta; Stephanie Wolfe Murray; John MacInnes; piper Alan MacDonald; Mary Beith of Melness; Donald Ease MacLeod; John Purser of Elgol; David Wilson; Robert Robertson of Pitlochry; Duncan Williamson of Furnace; Rebecca MacKay; Mary and Steve Acheson; Muriel and Caroline Neat and all staff at Birlinn – especially Hugh Andrew, Liz Short, Andrew Simmons, Mark Blackadder and Jim Hutcheson. And less directly, but crucially, I thank Carcanet Press, *The Daily Record* and *The Herald* for the use of material.

Donald MacLeod and John Cumming

ARNISH AND KYLE RONA

'It was like a swallow he was – flying over stooks'

The Two Wild Men of Rona – you will have heard of them, Alistair and Duncan MacLeod. They were men of enormous strength and build. Well I am descended from them, both on my father's side and my mother's side. They came from Screapadal, here on the island of Raasay. They were born around 1830 and in 1853 they were cleared by the landlord – Rainey was his name. They made their way north and got themselves new ground up on the island of Rona. It was one of them, Alistair, who built the wall at Hallaig, and he built the wall of Oskaig. You can still see those walls to this day, the sheep-pen and the cattle-fold. It was Alistair who built the wall and his brother's name was Duncan. It was after they got cleared and each got married to a woman that they became known as 'The Two Wild Men of Rona'. In 1851 the population of Rona was 115, in 1861 it was 144 – that was the newcomers coming in from Raasay. By 1891 the population was 181.

There's peat up there on Rona but the ground is solid gneis. There were too many people and not enough good ground. After that the population began to fall and in 1942 the last family, the MacRaes at Dryharbour, left. In 1978 the lighthouse went automatic and that was it. My mother, she was the granddaughter of the Two Wild Men. Every summer they walked to the fishings in the east coast. That's how they made a little bit of a livelihood. When I was young I was strong myself, but I never married. I've hardly ever left the island. So that's it.

You will have heard of the Raasay Raiders. My mother's father was one of them. My uncle at Eyre – he was a nephew of The Two Wild Men, the grandson of Duncan. He built the house I stay in today. They all came back to

Opposite.
Donald MacLeod of Arnish, Isle
of Raasay, 1997. (TN)

Donald MacDonald, outside his father's post office and ruined crofthouse, Arnish, North Raasay, 1998. (TN)

Raasay after the First World War. The MacKays in Fearns – they came in with the Raiders. So the Raasay men went up to Rona and waited, then they came back. They took back the ground from which they had been cleared, not from Rainey – he was long dead – but the Department of Agriculture. By the end of the Great War the Department of Agriculture owned the whole island of Raasay. The Raiders came down in boats and they said they would 'stay till the end of the world'. Soon enough they got sent to prison in Inverness and in Edinburgh. Things were hard, but they didn't return back empty-handed. They got good crofts on good ground and it's a strange thing – those Raiders missed a loop in the law – they might have got the whole island of Raasay! That's what I've heard.

I live down at Eyre at the south end but it's up here at Arnish I was born. This is the place I call home. My father ran the post office at Arnish. There were five postmen between Brochel Castle and Rona in those days. He had the croft here where we stand – ten acres. It's a very beautiful place, with the sun coming round in the evening. This is the place where I played as a child. I went to Torran school. The washing was hung on the birch trees to dry. There was a man stood here who had travelled the world and he said he knew no sight more lovely – looking across to Armishader, Tottrome, to the Storr. That's where the last sea-eagle was killed in 1916. There were plenty of people up here in those days, at Arnish, at

Torran, at Kyle Rona. There were three families on Eilean Fladda and one family on Eilean Tigh. Today there's no one here. There's a big salmon fishery in Loch Arnish but nobody living here since my cousin died – Calum MacLeod, 'Calum the Road'.

There must have been people living around the north end of Raasay for thousands of years, but it was the Clearances that increased the population here, just as it did on Rona. In many ways north Raasay was tied closer to Rona than it was to rest of Raasay. When the east Raasay townships at Hallaig and Screapadal were cleared, some families went to the mainland, some went abroad, some went to Rona and some came up to Arnish – but there were people cleared from Arnish itself. John MacLeod was sent away to Tasmania. He was a relative of mine. That was in 1853, not long after Rainey took over the island. He was a businessman from Edinburgh.

Rainey made his own laws – no horses on the island but his own. If the child of a tenant wanted to marry they had to leave the island. He was out to cut down numbers. If you had a brain he was keen to see the back of you. John MacLeod was the son of Malcolm MacLeod and his wife was Margaret. They were living at Leachd-Riabnach at Arnish. They had seven sons, two of whom were called John – Iain Mohr and Iain Beag. Iain Mhor went off to Nova Scotia – he emigrated – but Iain Beag got married and went into a crofthouse nearby his parents. Well, that was it, the news got back to Rainey. He wouldn't have it. He informed Iain Beag of the rules about marriage on the island but Iain Begg went on as before. Rainey then sent two of his men up from Raasay House. I heard all this myself from a very old man, Kenny MacLeod, back in the 'thirties. He was a boy of five when he saw the men coming up on two horses. He saw them taking things out of the house. They took a cradle with a new-born baby out onto the grass and they burnt the house to its walls. That was 1853 and after that Iain Beag, his wife and the baby got shipped out to Australia. They didn't want to go – few of the Raasay people wanted to go – but, to tell the truth, they did much better out there in Australia than if they'd stayed at Arnish. They got farms, big farms. My house down there at Eyre doesn't have basic facilities; no running water, no bathroom, no toilet, no electricity – not even a sink. It's damp to the roof. I've never had a car, nor a tractor; sometimes I don't see anybody for weeks on end. There's a lady comes down – she gives tea to elderly people once a month. And that's it.

I left Torran school when I was thirteen. I got my call-up papers for National Service in 1947, when I was eighteen. I was keen to go away and see more of the world but that year my father died and I had to stay on to run the croft. The Fladda boys – they did their National Service. It smartened them up; it did them good. I've been to Dingwall selling calves and cows. I've been to Inverness twice. When I was a boy we would get our messages by boat from

Top.
Donald MacLeod, Arnish, 1998.
(TN)

Bottom.
Donald MacLeod examines a boulder
split by lightening in the 1920s,
1998. (TN)

Opposite top and bottom.
Remnant of the corrugated shed that
Donald MacLeod built as a
young man, 1998. (TN)

Portree and now I'm hoping I'll get a move to Portree myself, into accommodation for the elderly. But I don't think I'm high on their list. In seventy years I've not seen much more of Skye than you can see from Raasay. Every day I look out on the Cuillin but I'm like a stranger to them in Portree. I've been to Edinbane. I was visiting my mother there when she was ill, and I was seeing my uncle when he grew old. Harrison Birtwistle, the composer – he used to be my nearest neighbour at Eyre. He had three boys. He used to say we had the most beautiful view in the world. But he's gone off away to live in France and I'm waiting to go into Portree.

My father was fifty-six when he died, and I was eighteen. He had been working stone all day. In the evening he complained of pains in his stomach, and later that night he complained of great pain. They telephoned the doctor in Portree but he didn't come. Next day he was worse. The doctor was called a second time. This time he did come – across by boat. When he got up to the house and saw my father he nearly collapsed. No tablets; nothing to kill the pain; a bucket of blood and vomit beside the bed. It was an ulcer in his stomach, a perforated ulcer it was that he had. The ulcer burst and he'd been vomiting all night. Well, the doctor ordered another boat and they took him away on a stretcher. They took him to Edinbane. That was the headquarters then. He never came round. It was October. He'd got this ulcer and nobody knew. I never heard him complain.

I liked working with my father. I remember that spring we'd had an awful lot of snow. My father and I, we used to go out feeding corn to the sheep and one day, on the way home, we caught three hares, the white hares. We dug them out of the snow. We'd watch them, chase them into a snowdrift then dig them out. It was June before the snow cleared from the hills of Storr. The bad winter,1947, we had no mail for six weeks. At last a boat came out from Lochaber. There were great icicles hung from the rocks, frozen waterfalls, like you see in the encyclopaedia.

The ground at Arnish is steep but there was good deep soil and it was fertile. The fields went down like terraces between the birches. There's more wood now. Each croft had access to common grazing. We had wood, we had peat, but there was no road out of Arnish; no road out. Everything had to come in by boat and everything had to be carried up from the shore. That was because the landlord, Wood – he was the best of the Raasay landlords – insisted that the house was built not on the shore, where he might wish to fish or picnic, but two-thirds up the hillside, where the house, with its smoke, would look good from the sea. I've seen myself carrying a boll of oatmeal up here so many times. I would stop for one rest, half way, but then carry on with no pause. That's half a mile, up 600 feet. It's the kind of thing you do when you are young and it's the kind of thing will come back at you when you're old. But we didn't think about that, arthritis, ruptures. We were used to it, trained to it. Right up to the steps of the house I carried that load on my back, 140 pounds. One time I decided to double the task, to carry the boll the whole way without stopping. And I did it. We had to carry lime, we had to carry slate; we had to carry all the wood, galvanised iron. Up from the shore. People speak against galvanised iron and corrugated roofs but for us they came as a Godsend. We painted the galvanise red or green or blue and even today I think the rust looks good, in its way. So that's it. My grandfather had wanted to build the house near the shore, but the proprietor wouldn't hear of it. He had a yacht and he wanted a view of the houses as he passed in his boat on his way up to Rona. Sunday afternoon.

Things were hard but looking out you'd always see someone. Someone working; someone out in a boat; the postmen coming up the paths from below. Things were quiet. We didn't like to shout. These rocks carry sound like a megaphone so we didn't shout at all in North Arnish. We didn't need to shout. We could see each other; we knew the signals. I can see her now, my mother, waving the white tea cloth, calling us for tea. Working with the *cas crom*, or the sickle, we'd stop and look up and see her waving. No need to shout. And up we'd go. And down at Eyre by myself, if I go into the wood, I still hear my grandmother calling – me playing on the rocks – 'Careful on those rocks, Donald!' I hear her now: not shouting, but calling, wanting to let me know she was there.

My father was the postman and our house was the Arnish Post Office. So if, when he was working the croft, there was a telephone message for the people at Torran, or on Fladda, or if our boat was needed on Rona, my mother would place the white cloth on the hill. That was the signal. A white cloth on the hill. I see it yet. My father would straighten, put a hand through his hair, and go back. Maybe not a word would be said. Sometimes I'd go with him and sometimes I'd stay. We grew corn. A big job was cutting grass, cutting the hay, with sickles; and in the evening I would take his sickle, with mine, up to the house.

There were three children. I was the oldest, my brother was the youngest. My sister was happy as long as she was tending the cows. She's like that to this day – anything to do with cows and she's happy. We were keeping three cows for milk and three followers. They wandered free for most of the year. Milking time they'd be down in the birch wood and they'd see us coming and they'd stand for us. No byre, no halter; they knew us and when they saw us they'd come up chewing their cud and stand to be milked. In the winters they came inside; they were petted, they had their own stalls, they were like members of the family.

My mother was very good at making butter and cream and scones and things like that. And if people came – visitors in the summer – she'd give them a tumbler of cream – natural cream – and it was good. People on holiday

Harvesting, Arnish, 1930s.
(TN/DM)

would come up to the post office to talk and post letters and cards. My mother enjoyed talking with them. Crowdie, curds and whey and all the things like that she made. Brose. What people were eating on Raasay then was food with great substance in it and it gave you strength. Porridge, fish, mutton. We were not buying anything. Especially when the rations were on. Months might pass and we buy nothing. We ate fish and salted fish; we grew potatoes and vegetables. If you had £5 then, it would last you months.

I used to say that I would never move out of Arnish. I was saying this to others and to myself, 'I'll see all you others go before I move out of here!' I was young and that's what I truly thought – 'I'll never leave this place.' But the wheel turned very suddenly. My father died, the post dried up; more and more everybody needed money. And my sister was keen on getting married. It was difficult for the women here then. The name of her man was Charlie – John MacLeod was his real name – and he was always coming away up here to see her. She wanted to go with him. Four years he came before we left and two years after we left they were married. Now we're all getting old, but they've got their three daughters. One's in Tain – Dolina – she's a graphic designer; one works with the BBC in Ullapool – that's Morag. And there's Wilma – she's named after my brother who was drowned. They're women now but not one of them is married.

The Arnish people were always going away. My grandfather would be going to Wick for the herring fishing. A small gang of them would walk. The railways had hardly begun then. And at the end of the season he'd come home with money in his pocket. Twelve pounds my grandmother said was the best he brought home, but that was a lot in those days. We had a garden and a sycamore tree and the washing was hung on the birches down there. It was beautiful, lovely. We'd sit outside of a summer evening. Sometimes somebody would come to post a letter and talk.

The house was stone with a roof of Ballachulish slate. Very heavy slates. Inside, my father lined the whole house with wood. After the condemnation order was passed on the house, the man from the Department said he'd never dismantled a house in such good condition. Red pine – no woodworm, no dry rot, nothing. They took out everything but the walls so no one could go back. I remember it all as being so cosy. When we were young they put us into a closet, but later on we'd sleep just anywhere, near the fire or against the wall in blankets or a plaid. We had a garret. My grandmother had her own room. It was she who would do all the baking. Never once did I hear her complain. She had no arthritis or pain in her legs. They were very good these old ladies then. She was a Nicolson from Rona and a MacKay. So that was it.

Donald MacLeod's father and mother, Arnish postmaster and mistress, c.1940. (DM)

When my father died all the responsibilities fell on my shoulders. The post up to Rona was finished; there was nobody up there but the lighthouse men. The MacRaes at Dryharbour were the last to leave. Two brothers and a sister – they went down to Kyleakin. They just let things go. I was up there once and they had a log on the fire but the end of the log came out through the door. They slowly moved the log in as the end burned away. We just had to do our best. My mother slowly became an invalid. Things went downhill. By the late 'fifties everybody but us, and my cousin Calum MacLeod – Calum the Road – had left the north end. He was servicing the lighthouse but at that time he hadn't started building his road, so we were dependent on the boats, and even a small boat can be heavy. Our house was condemned and we were persuaded to move down to Eyre at the south end of the island. Then, because I'd left the house I had to let the croft go. We got compensation but now, of course, I wish I'd hung on to our right to the croft, to the ground, but I was down there at the other end of the island and the Crofting Commission had different regulations then. All the official bodies wanted us out, that's why they put down the condemnation order. I offered to buy the house – but once a house has been condemned there's nothing you can do about it. I said to the Department of Agriculture, 'This is a fine house, if you want to condemn a house you should condemn the Rona lighthouse house, not this one! There's no water or electricity up there at the lighthouse. There's no difference between facilities here and facilities there, this is a good house,' I said. But they wanted men up at the lighthouse in those days and didn't want people here. So they went ahead and tore down what was a substantial dwelling. So that was it. We came out in 1958.

On and off I kept fighting the Department for about half a dozen years. And, though I didn't know it, there were things going on behind my back. Now the whole place belongs to Nicolson, the big fellow, in Torran. He's got everything that we had; the school, all the Torran ground and more besides. And with Calum MacLeod gone, it's the Nicolsons have got the whole place. They've even got the ground where Lexie's sheep still graze – that's Calum's widow. She lives down above the Raasay pier. You see, Nicolson was an ex-serviceman and ex-servicemen were being offered crofts and the like of that and he worked in the Lighthouse Service. So the Nicolsons prospered and I wish them well.

My mother lived for eleven years after we left Arnish. She died in November 1969. My brother Willie – he went away in the Admiralty Service. He was here at my mother's funeral that November and he stayed at home till the New Year. Then he went away back down to Wales, to Milford Haven, and he was drowned. We got his remains. He was buried in Raasay. He was thirty-two years of age. There was a Harris man with him when he died; he tried his best to rescue him but he had no chance. Willie was working on the boat when he slipped. As he fell his forehead must have struck the gunnel. They wrote to say there was a massive bruise on his forehead and it was likely he would have been unconscious before he hit the water. He was trapped down there between the pier and the boat, under the water. In about an hour he was up, but too late. The Harris man jumped in with a lifebelt but he couldn't get in to him. The Admiralty sent us photographs of how the ladders were fixed to the pier to show us where and how he must have fallen. So, that was it. He was brought home by road through the Seven Sisters of Kintail. I look on them every time I go out to the shed. We waited as the ferry brought him back from Sconser. The water was grey and the snow was white on the Cuillin, but the Skye mountains were not the last thing that he saw – that would have been the gunnel and the side of the ship.

This is my first visit up to the north end for three years. It's Nicolsons here now – they run big flocks of sheep. If my great grandfathers were alive they'd go mad! If they were to hear there were eight Nicolsons in Torran, rounding-up sheep, they'd go mad. Well, well, well. Nicolsons and MacLeods, there was something queer about it. These Highlanders were strong men – very strong men – they'd always be testing, always quarrelling among themselves. Landlords weren't the only problem – brothers would fight, cousins would fight. I've seen it myself. Things were tight you see. Money was tight. The stronger man had the upper hand. If I was stronger than you, I'd have the upper hand.

I heard about these Nicolsons from my father, and I heard about their ancestors. They were repairing a fence up here at Arnish and my

MacLeod family group, Arnish Post Office, c.1945. (DM)

·Donald's sisters, with new stockings, outside the Arnish (and Torran) post office, 1950. (DM)

grandfather's brother was doing something on his grandfather's croft. And the Nicolsons were out up above him, they were fencing the hill, and they were shouting and they shouted down, 'Come up and give us a hand!' because that fence was the boundary between them and the work was there to be shared. Well, my grand-uncle didn't like shouting but he shouted back 'Go home! And put your head in a pot of urine!' There was a feud between those families then. We didn't like the Nicolsons.

I heard there was a Nicolson once, Murdo Nicolson, fishing on the east coast when a big Negro came ashore off one of the boats and he saw this

Donald MacLeod's brother William (right) with friend, c.1965. William was drowned in Milford Haven in 1969. (DM)

Nicolson, and he went straight up to him and he said 'Hullo brother, when did you come over?' That Nicolson was like a Negro as a man can be – curly matted hair, thick lips and all that – and this negro thought he was a real Negro! There's one of them in Portree yet, a Charlie Nicholson, he was brought up over there. Of course there were Nicolsons in amongst my grandmother's people. We used to say that a black man came ashore at Rona once, long, long ago and it was off him the Nicolsons come down! Well, well, well, we'll never know who we are!

And you will have heard of another Nicolson – Ewan Nicolson – who was seen flying over stooks on Rona. He was swooping over the corn stooks and standing on them like a bird. Perched. He was seen doing this by the man who built my house down at Eyre – Donald MacLeod – a first cousin of my mother's. Now Donald was a very religious man and when he realised what Ewan Nicolson was up to, he went to the window with his Bible. He placed the book on the window sill and there, before that field of stooks, he let the pages flutter in the wind and he read the word of God as the pages turned. This was done to assuage the evil he had seen and later, when he met Ewan, he said to him 'I have seen you. I have watched you flying over stooks like a bird – such powers are not natural. You are a substantial man with a body. Let me never catch you swooping like a bird again. Let that be the last of it!' I remember both men very well, though both were dead before I left Arnish. Donald said it was like a swallow he was, flying over the stooks.

Ewan Nicolson was a man who had that 'spirit' in him; he liked to give a shock. He was known here as 'Turcay', that means 'The Trickster' but it wasn't just tricks that he did, he had other powers. One night in the spring, he was singing in this house when suddenly he stopped, in the middle of a word, and he rushed from the room and did not return. In the morning the news went round and people went looking for him. And there they found him, high on the cliffs on the west side of Rona, halfway to the lighthouse, where the scarts and seabirds have their nests. He had climbed where no natural man could climb, high up above sprung rocks which overhang and where there is no place to put your legs. Well, there he was walking with his bonnet in his hand, collecting eggs, singing the last verse of the song. And later on he lowered baskets full of eggs down to those who had found him.

One day when the Rona people were going over to Portree in the boat, a sailing boat, he disappeared; suddenly he went missing. There was a shout 'Where's Ewan! Man overboard! Man overboard!' And the boat was swung round and sailed back along its wake. Everybody was searching the water for a sign of the man. Nothing was found. Knowing Ewan Nicolson was a trickster they made a last search of the boat. Nothing. But as they moved into Portree harbour his head came over the side – there he was crouched beneath the bowsprit, balanced on two small hooks, invisible.

It was said he kept a diary, noting down his tricks and how to do them, and these were both natural and unnatural, big and small. One day one of the Rona men was coming back form Portree with a new pair of Wellington boots, so, for devilment, Ewan crept up behind, underneath the seats, and with a very sharp knife he punctured the boots. That man didn't feel a thing, but when he stepped ashore at Rona he gave out a cry: 'These boots are leaking! New boots!' Nobody knew who did, not for years – it was only later on that they realised who it was who had done it. Another time he went away to the mainland

Donald examines a tree he used to play on as a child, 1999. (TN)

and he came back with a rubber mouth and suddenly he blew his tongue out to a gigantic length, till it burst. Then he did it again. It was bubblegum, but people didn't know about these things on Rona, or about the tricks you buy in shops. But, more than that, Ewan Nicolson had special powers – he had the power of mesmerising people. He liked to put a fear in people. At a ceilidh he would suddenly double up and cry out 'I've got a ball of hay stuck in my stomach!' He'd be rolling in agony and he'd get people to lay him out on a bed, and he'd get a woman to tie his legs up over his head to ease the pain. He was a single man, then he got married. He married his first cousin. No one else would have him!

You'll know the Giant's Cave on Rona. They used to have church services in there, with little rows of stones for seats. Well, there was a great Bible left in that cave for years and years, till the historians took it away. And one day Ewan Nicolson was seen visiting the cave, and after he had gone others went in, and they found this book, this diary, wedged in between two stones, where the children sat. They couldn't understand or make head nor tail of what was in it — drawings and writings — so they took it back to one of the houses and they burned it. And I've heard that book went off with a bang that almost put the house on fire. It seems it was the power of black magic that Ewan had, when he was young.

But when I knew him he was a man of great silences. He would hardly say a word at all, for hours on end, but he still had a great power of the mind. He could mesmerise you even then. He collected winkles and he sold them in Portree, and all the children – he would want them to kiss him. He would stand in the street looking at a girl, wanting to be kissed by her, and the tears would be running down his cheeks, waiting, waiting for the kisses, and the girl would run on down the street. But he had that power, so much power, that at last the girl would come back, come up to him and kiss him. Only then would he move on. Many's the time I would sit with him. He would be in his chair. And he would look so sad. He would look so sad if I started looking at him, and he would look at me, but not a word would come out of his mouth and the tears would be falling down his face. And the only thing he would ask would be for me to put a peat or two on the fire before I left.

Well, that was it. The old people here then, when they saw or heard of the things that Ewan Nicolson did, would say, 'That's witchery, that's witchcraft.' That's it. That's all I know about Ewan Nicolson. Strange things went on in the old days and strange things are still going on. I've heard they're expecting a new warden at the youth hostel. That's three in no time. The last man was from Liverpool, a very nice man. And before that there was a woman from Loch Lomond, a nice Lowland woman, and my cousin Willie, at Eyre – he went and married her! He courted her and he married her and they were together for ten years – then, one day, she disappeared! Four years he'd spent building their house. Then, as soon as it was finished, she said she was going on her holiday to her mother's, and she never came back! She never mentioned to Willie she was going to stay away. But that man never again saw his wife in Raasay! She was an awful nice woman. Her father was a forester. She took the children. Willie went down to Loch Lomond but they wouldn't let him in the house! You'd think something dreadful must have happened! However it's all turned out well. He's got another woman, a Spanish woman from Raasay House, and we hear his old wife is very happy away down there by Loch Lomond. The only thing I'd say is that he doesn't look after his sheep as well as he might.

Sir Harrison Birtwistle, the composer – he was my neighbour at Eyre for years. He was a very quiet man: he kept himself to himself. He had three boys – they went away to school in England. Now he's moved to France. He had a beautiful view of the Clarach and the Cuillin from his studio here, but out there, I've heard, he works with his face to the wall and his window looks out onto a planted hedge. He said, 'Having looked on the Cuillin, I know nothing can match them. My going from here is like a bereavement – but Raasay is still there in my music, as much as my parents are here in my hand.' And that was it, we haven't seen him since.

I told you about Calum the Road. He wrote a book called *The Great Men of Raasay*. It's very good but he forgot to put me in – and himself! That's a joke. He was my cousin. He was the last man to come out of Arnish, South Arnish. His brother, Charlie, still lives in Portree, with their sister. He was called Calum the Road because it was he built the road out of Arnish, and into Arnish. The pity was it came too late for the people who lived there.

Calum was born in Glasgow but he came back to his grandfather's croft when the war broke out in 1914. In 1927 he joined my father on the Rona Lighthouse attending boat. When my father died, Calum became Boatman-in-Charge and he tended the lighthouse for twenty years till, in 1967, he got his Lighthouse-Keeper certificate and was appointed Local Assistant at the Rona Light. Well, after that he worked one month on and one month off, so what he decided to do was to build a road out of Arnish in his months off. With a road he hoped new generations of people would return to Arnish and all the north end of Raasay. There were 10,000 acres of ground, sheltered bays and good fishing, but only Calum and his wife up there at all.

Petitions had been sent up to Inverness for years and years but nothing was done. So it was that Calum decided to build the road himself. From Torran to Arnish and Arnish to Brochel Castle. Maybe it's only three miles but it

Donald MacLeod, Arnish, 1999.
(TN)

was rough, mountainous terrain and the road had to be cut against the fall of the ground. It was a big job for one man. But Calum bought a book, *Road Making and Maintenance – a Practical Treatise for Engineers, Surveyors and Others*, by Thomas Aitkin. Calum was one of the 'others'! The book cost him twenty-five pence and he started in the summer of 1966. He got extra advice from two Army engineers – Major Mitcham and Captain Harrison – and, after he got started, the Department of Agriculture gave him a compressor, a driller, a blaster and explosives as he needed them. For transportation of materials he had only a wheelbarrow, but from the start he worked to make a real road, a road for motor vehicles. It was not a track for hikers that he built. So, one morning in June, Lexie packed his lunchbox – she'd been the schoolteacher down at Torran school – and off he set for Brochel Castle. Cutting trees was his first job and it was an easy job but getting out the roots was one of the hardest. The first day on a job is often

*Calum MacLeod building the road
from Arnish to Brochel Castle
(1966–76). (GH)*

Left.
Calum MacLeod of Arnish, crofter,
lighthouse man and road builder,
c.1984. (CS)

Right.
Calum MacLeod holds up a Neolithic
axe-head found whilst digging his
road, c.1975. (GH)

the worst but Calum wouldn't give in. He was fifty-five and he had a plan for the rest of his life – to work at the Brochel end through the summer, when the days were long, and to work at the Arnish end in the wintertime, and not to stop till the road was finished. He laid foundations twelve feet wide for a ten-foot surface road. He had a crowbar. He wore out three wheelbarrows, six picks, six shovels, five big hammers and four spades. The biggest boulder he shifted weighed, they say, nine tons. He built drystane embankments, and where the burns ran across the road he built stone culverts on top of flagstones and these were cushioned with faggots of birchwood where the ground was peat. Not far south of Arnish he broke down the wall with which Rainey had enclosed his sheep-tack in 1854. I imagine a big cheer went up in his heart when he did that.

Well, Calum worked for ten years on the road. If I'd still been up at Arnish I would have helped him myself. Many's the building up there we built together when I was young – but with the croft down at Eyre I had no chance of helping up here on the road. And in 1976, the year Calum retired from the lighthouse, the road was finished. Cars, trucks and tractors could now get through. With just two people and one croft at the end the road was hardly used but Calum had set the ball rolling and in 1982 Highland Regional Council decided to take over the road. They brought in machinery, they put down Tarmacadam and they upgraded the road to a highway with passing places and it stops just 350 yards short of Calum's house. So that was it. That's Calum the Road.

Now we have a good road but we still have no people. Calum lived for another six years. He had a heart attack when he was out by the sheds. Lexie

Right.
Calum MacLeod cutting hay, Arnish,
1984. (CS)

Opposite.
John Cumming of Kyle Rona and
Inverarish, 1998. (TN)

found him half-sitting and half-lying like, a great big baby in his wheelbarrow. He must have fallen, or perhaps he knew that his end had come and he went to the wheelbarrow and lay down in it to die. Lexie phoned for the doctor, but by the time he got over from Portree, *rigor mortis* was well set in. His life and his death were shaped by his wheelbarrow. Calum was the last man to come out of Arnish, down the road he built with his hands.

JOHN CUMMING – KYLE RONA

My great-grandfather was the herd on Fladda – that's the big island on the west side of Raasay between Torran and Kyle Rona. He came from Skye and he brought his family over. Later on my grandfather took a croft on Eilean Tigh, further north. He was king of the island. There was one house! It's half a mile south-west of Rona, but it's a tidal island on the Raasay side – just forty yards offshore. My own father crofted at Eilean Tigh, but towards the end he had a croft on the mainland at Kyle Rona. Caol Rona is the name of the Kyle between Raasay and Rona, but was also the name of the last township up there at the north end of Raasay. It was good crofting ground. That's were I was born in 1915 – Kyle Rona.

On the Ordnance Survey maps the crofthouse and the boatsheds on Eilean Tigh are marked down as sheilings. That's wrong. And all the crofthouses and byres at Kyle Rona are marked down as sheilings; that's also wrong. There are no sheilings at the north end of Raasay; they were all crofthouses and buildings for permanent use. There were six families up there when I was young. That would mean about fifty people. It was after the First World War that the numbers went down and by the time of the Second World War the whole population had dwindled away.

Our family was the last to leave Kyle Rona. I was twenty-eight. It's just rushes and bracken and rough ground today. It's a long walk for a man of my age, five miles beyond the end of Calum's road. The path was never good, not much more than a sheep track. Being up there brings back so many memories. I've not been for four years. It's not nice to see everything derelict. Every single person gone. All vanity.

Further south, people hung on at North Arnish but Donald MacLeod and his family went away in 1958 and Calum MacLeod built the road to no avail. All vanity. There's nobody left. I was at Torran school with Calum; he was always very clever. He won a gold medal for Gaelic. He was very well read. He was always sending off letters to the newspapers. The *West Highland Free Press* used to rely on him! He was a distant relative of Sorley Maclean, the poet. I'm a relative of Sorley's as well. He used to come here to talk with me. And his brothers. Of the five brothers there's just one left. I have Sorley's books and a photograph on my table. You'll know the poem, 'Hallaig'.

> They are still in Hallaig
> MacLeans and MacLeods
> all who were there in the time of Mac Gille Chaluim
> the dead have been seen alive.
>
> The men lying on the green
> At the end of every house that was,
> the girls a wood of birches,
> straight their backs, bent their heads.

My grandfather was a bard and he was a king! We all liked the King of the Island. Coming home from school he'd be there, sitting outside the house, waiting for us. He was over seventy. He'd been in the Royal Naval Reserve and seen service on the *Royal Sovereign*. He used to show us boys the naval drill, how to load and fire the big guns. We'd march up and down on the green. He'd be shouting out the orders, whistling the tunes. He used to sing – he was a very good singer – and he made many songs. It was all Gaelic with us but very few of us could read or write Gaelic, so all his songs are lost, or almost all. I remember one about the Boer War: he made it himself.

Torran school was a long way from Eilean Tigh. If the tide was out we crossed to Kyle Rona on foot; if the tide was in we took the rowing boat. Then we had a walk of four miles. The hills at the north end are not high but it's rough country. There was no road – there was hardly a track – just rough stones and heather and peat bog. Because we lived far out, we didn't have to be in school till about ten o'clock. We stayed till four. We didn't get a piece at breaktime; we didn't get any dinner. By the time we got home in the evenings we'd be starving. Hunger kept us from hanging about! In wintertime, three days in four we'd have rain.

My mother was Sheila Nicolson. She had seven children. I was the second son. I had an older brother, Murdo, but he died when he was fourteen. After me came five sisters. Our teacher was Seamus Mohr from Glendale on the Isle of Skye. He was very, very lame. He was not a qualified teacher, he was an exciseman. He'd fallen into the hold of a ship and broken his hip. He always had a walking stick. He had Gaelic, as we had Gaelic, but the teaching was all in English. We had a Gaelic reader and we had Gaelic singing but we didn't study in Gaelic, nor did we learn Gaelic grammar. We also had Miss Reid from Kyleakin. She didn't have Gaelic. We learned English so we'd get on in the world. It's a strange thing but the only English spoken at Kyle Rona was for the dogs. Every house had a dog up there for the sheep. We called them Fly, Mouldie, Toddie, names like that – Bracken, Fern – and all the command was in English. Why would that be? Would that be because the shepherds were often men who'd come up from the border, from the Lowlands? You see them on television – *One Man and His Dog*. Tremendous control those shepherds have of their dogs. But it was cattle, not sheep that we had, and with cattle you didn't really need dogs. With plenty of people you don't really need to train dogs. And the names of many of our cows would also be English.

The postal service was very important to us in Kyle Rona. Not only did most things come by post, but the post office gave steady employment. There were five postmen at the north end of Raasay. My father was the postman for Rona. Twice a week he'd go down to North Arnish to pick up the mail. If he had more than thirty-five pounds to carry, I'd get paid as assistant postman. We carried the mail in big packs strapped on our backs. Twice a week we'd cross the Kyle, one man on each oar, around the back of nine. Then it was a six miles' walk north to the lighthouse, delivering letters, parcels and papers as we went. No roads. We'd be there by dinnertime and back to the Kyle by four o'clock.

As time went on there was less and less post – except for the lighthouse men. When I was a boy there were still plenty of people on Rona. There were sixty children in the school at Dry Harbour at one time. And there was another school at Doire na Guaile down at our end. There was a church on Rona. They had big services in the church, and in the Great Cave where Maighstair Ruari preached and the people sat on stones. The MaCraes were the last inhabitants. Years before they'd come to Rona from Kintail. They had a big croft at Dry Harbour. In the end there were just two brothers and a sister left, unmarried. In 1942 they went away down to Kyleakin – that was one year before

DELIVERING HIS MAJESTY'S MAIL.

Kyle Rona postman, c.1920. (WM)

we left Kyle Rona. It was the domino theory in practice.

Christmas time was the busy time for post here, like everywhere else, but the weather could be very bad at the turn of the year. A nor'westerly gale was the worst. Just like the children at school, my father would eat nothing through the day. He might get a cup of tea at the lighthouse, but normally we had nothing but a drink at the spring till we got back to Raasay. Sandwiches were unheard of in those days. It's only half a mile but Caol Rona will stack up in a storm – there are shallow waters in there. Many's the day we couldn't cross. One day, rowing home from Port am Teampuill, I remember a big wave coming back off a skerry and swamping the boat, up to our knees, almost up to the gunnel. No lifebelts in those days. We had to bail for our lives.

Wintertime was the quiet time. It was April when the croft work got started. The *cas chrom* came out and the creels. The oats and potatoes would be planted. We had no tractors, no horses, no oxen, no camels! Nothing! Everything was done by hand. I've read that there was once one horse on Rona, but I didn't see any kind of horse till I went by boat to Portree when I was seven years old. On Eilean Tigh we had three cows and three followers. At Kyle Rona we had more. We had cabbages. We went out after fish. We fished with nets, long lines and arrows – that's the feathered hooks. There were plenty of fish then but not now. Conger eels – we used to get plenty of them. In a rowing boat they can

be dangerous. I remember one locking onto the foot of my wellington. The teeth went through like a razor, shaving my socks but missing my toes! We used to try to kill them as soon as they came over the side with a baton. We had plenty fresh fish. We salted herring and haddock. When we got lobsters, we tried to get them to market.

Lighthouse men and two visitors, Kyle Rona, c.1938. (DM)

In May, with the good weather, we'd start cutting the peat, stacking them in the May wind and the sun. Then we'd make a big *cruich* – that's a thick wall of peat-slabs – with turfs on the top to keep out the rain. All our peat was more than two miles distant. It was left there, on the hill. It was our custom to bring home peat in creels, every day through the year. Almost every day. Some people built a peat-stack near the house but not us. The walk to the peats was something we did: the daily round the common task. The good peat had been used up at Kyle Rona by our time, gradually we had to go further and further south, till we met the Arnish people coming north! Three miles in the end.

We saw few outsiders at Kyle Rona, just one or two hikers. For weeks we'd see no one. In the summer the tinkers used to come over to Raasay on the Sconser Ferry, and they came right up to Arnish, to Kyle Rona, to Eilean Tigh, and they'd ask us to take them over to Rona. They were Stewarts. They slept out, they sold things that they made and things that they'd bought cheap on the mainland. There was nowhere the tinkers didn't go in those days.

Life was good but it was little more than subsistence: my father needed me on the croft but as soon as my sisters left school they went away to work on the mainland. There was nothing for them at Kyle Rona. When I got into my twenties we got ourselves a motorboat. We used to cross to Portree to bring in winter stores; three or four bolls of meal, hardware, oil, diesel; but basically, Kyle Rona was self-sufficient. We made what we needed and we ate what we grew or what we caught. For breakfast it was brose and porridge. Twice a week we would eat cormorants. We shot them off the rocks. We skinned them, we made broth with them, we stewed them, and had them with oatmeal. Some people say they're fishy to taste but that's because they haven't eaten them or not cooked them the right way. Cormorants and shags —we call them 'scart' — can be very good. People don't like to think of birds being eaten — except for chicken and turkeys and pheasants and grouse. On Lewis they still eat the *guga* — that's the solan goose, the gannet — but that was not usual with us. However we had a Raasay man married to a Lewis girl and she used to bring them over. Every year the men would go up to North Rona and bring back thousands of birds to sell on the shore up at Ness. They're very good. We enjoyed them. We shot wild duck. We had few rabbits but plenty of snow hares. We made crowdie, curds and whey. We used to make nettle soup and we made a drink from nettles. And we made soup from dulce, the seaweed.

We weren't short of meat. When we killed a beast it would usually be shared amongst four families. Most of the beef would be salted; lamb would be salted. The day a beast was to be killed was a big day with us — we'd all gather for the slaughter. The work would be done out in the open and afterwards we'd have a dram. White puddings were made; black puddings. We didn't drink much in those days, just a beer and a dram at New Year. And a ceilidh with us would be a quiet affair. I learned the mouth organ. I don't play the pipes but I know pipe-music. If a piper was to start up outside, I'd tell you the tune he was playing. I can do that. Sorley's brother John could do that. Sound any three notes of a *pibroch* and he could tell you from which *pibroch* they came.

We'd keep a good milking cow for years but we'd be selling the calves. People would come across from the Wills Estate at Applecross, the tobacco people. They'd come with a big boat into the harbour at Fladda. Four pounds for a stirk they paid. Lambs were driven down to Raasay pier.

Camp coffee was a favourite drink with us, with the Indian Scotsman there on the bottle! Tea would come by post from Edinburgh, from MacLeods, that was a family with Skye connections going back to the bard Neil MacLeod. All that kind of stuff — tea, coffee, sugar — was brought in by mail. Clothes would come by mail order. That was one reason why the postbags were heavy — that's why we needed five postmen!

John Cumming gardening at Osgaig,
Raasay, 1998. (TN)

J. D. Williams in Manchester! The name gives a lift to my heart. They used to send out a catalogue. J. D. Williams, Dale Street, Manchester. I remember the address to this day. The promise was 'One week or ten days by return'. 12/6 for a pair of shoes, 12/6 for a bottle of whisky:

> Twelve and a tanner a bottle –
> That's what it's costing today!
> Twelve and a tanner a bottle –
> It takes all the pleasure away!
>
> Just to get a wee drop
> I've got to spend all I've got –
> Oh what it is to be happy
> When happiness costs such a lot!

In a subsistence economy big families put a strain on subsistence. And the families at Kyle Rona were big. When children left school, they left Raasay. There was no paid work for them here on the island. Girls would go into service, or into nursing. The boys would go away to Glasgow and join what we called 'the Skye Navy' on the Clyde – they'd be working as dockers and stevedores. Some would

join the army, the navy, the merchant navy. All my uncles were farm workers on the Black Isle in Easter Ross. Because I was working the crofts, when the war came I was in a reserved occupation but I didn't want to stay up at Kyle Rona, with me being the only man under sixty, so in 1942 I joined the Ordnance Corps. Fours years I was away – till 1946 – all over England, Normandy, France, Belgium and Germany. I hardly saw a Gael the whole time I was away but it was a good experience for me and when I came out I stayed in the Volunteer Reserve. I was not directly involved in any fighting – we were sending up ammunition, road building, mapping, building huts with the Royal Engineers, all that kind of thing. It was in 1943 that my father and mother came away from Kyle Rona and the whole north end left deserted.

Like Calum the Road and Donald MacLeod, I would have loved to have stayed and kept those old communities going – so many good people lived in those places and came out of those places. But professors and doctors – they had to go away. There was a woman in Kyle Rona whose name was Peggy Beaton. She came from Skye to marry a Gillies and she brought a great knowledge of plants and medicine and she acted as the local chemist for us. She was descended from the famous Beatons who came from France to be physicians to the Lords of the Isles way back in the Middle Ages, and it's been said that that family, for generations, knew more about medicine than any other family in the whole of Britain. Well, Peggy Beaton was our next door neighbour and I remember going into her wee thatched cottage and seeing the rows of jars – full of leaves and seeds and coloured sticks. She had special leaves you put onto a cut, dried herbs and oils. She wasn't a doctor but she had all kinds of information about plants and cures, all handed down. She had six children but they went away and she and her husband went away too. The movement of people. It was a great tragedy for Sorley MacLean. I look on him as spokesman for the Raasay people:

> Screapadal the sheep-pen and the cattle-fold
> with walls to the south and west and north,
> and to the east sea sound
> over to the sanctuary of Maol Rubha.
> There is a half dead memory of Maol Rubha
> but only the dead written names
> of the children, men and women
> whom Rainy put off the land
> between the north end of the rock
> and the castle built for MacSwan
> or for MacGille-Chaluim
> for violence and refuge …
>
> Rainy, who cleared fourteen townships
> in the island of the Big Men,
> Great Raasay of the MacLeods.

Fourteen townships. Fourteen Raasay men fell at the Battle of Culloden. After that the Hanoverians sent troops here and they ravaged the place. They took sheep and cattle just as they needed. Some of the houses were burned. But its a strange thing, the population of Raasay went on rising all through the eighteenth century and through the nineteenth century – even through the worst years of the Clearances. People were hounded up to Rona and the north end of Raasay. Those were terrible days, but it is the twentieth century that has seen the native population of Rona and Raasay shrink almost to nothing. The people have gone from Kyle Rona, from Torran, from Arnish, from Fladda, from Eilean Tigh, from Rona – all this in my day. The population of Skye is now going back up, but Raasay – what will happen to Raasay?

Lachie Morrison of Grimsay

HEISKER AND GRIMSAY, NORTH UIST

'And the Turks will be swept from the tops of the mountains.'

My father was Patrick Morrison. He was crofter, a fisherman and a bard. He was away four years in the First World War. He was at Gallipoli, he was at Salonika, he was in France. He saw terrible things and experienced terrible things and he was always thinking of North Uist. He wrote a poem in Salonika in 1916 and it was all about home. It goes to a very powerful tune and he used to sing it to us here in Grimsay. My brother used to sing it and people still ask me to sing it today. All my father's songs were composed and kept in his head. He took all the songs of his youth away with him to the war and in the run of things out there he must have lost some. If you don't sing you lose the best of your voice and even a bard, if he doesn't sing his songs, will forget. Only one song of all the songs composed by my father was written down before the year of his death – that was when Donald Archie MacDonald came from the school of Scottish Studies and he got my father to sing as many as he could remember, and Donald Archie took them down for publication in a book. The words and the tunes. It's fantastic, really, that he remembered so many. This is his 'Song of War', sent home from Salonika. It should be sung to the tune: 'Bu chaomh leam bhith 'mire'.

> Drink health to the lads whom Lovat recruited
> Drink health to the lads whom Lovat recruited;
> My dearest wish is their safe return –
> For so many of us here belong to Uist of the beinns.

Opposite.
Lachie Morrison, Grimsay, North Uist, 1997. (TN)

Above left.
Patrick and Flora Morrison, c.1925.
They resettled on Heisker with their
four children in 1945. (LM)

Above right.
Lachie Morrison's mother, Flora, and
elder sister, Annie, c.1940. (LM)

Menfolk now at home who ceilidh the houses,
Relaying the news as it comes in from France,
Each warm and at ease around the peat fire –
I would willing be with you at this moment in time!

It's so different with me and the rest of the lads
As we stand drenched in a downpour of ungiving rain,
In a hail of Turkish gunfire, bullets and shells,
That thunder down in a deluge on everyman's head.

Though I'm allotted a slot of time in my blanket –
I'm no sooner asleep, not even starting to snore,
When orders come down from the Colonel. 'Stand Firm!
Prepare to repel imminent attack!'

When battle begins the noise is stormforce in our ears
The very ground all around begins to tremble beneath us;
But the lads stand undaunted with their guns to their
Shoulders – Drop dead the bastards and victory is ours!

The bullets and shrapnel fly in plenty around us
Unpleasant the whine as metal screams past us –
Lads who were stalwart fall wordless beside us
And bayonets fixed for close-quarter battle.

So different to when I was young and out sailing,
Together with Donald, who was my best friend,
Our guns clean-polished and my dog on the floorboards –
Swimming out to retrieve every bird that we shot.

But – I must not complain or be nostalgic in verse!
I will stand shoulder to shoulder with the hardiest Gaels
Who have ever in battle stood firm to win Honour
And the Turks will be swept from the tops of the mountains.

Our hope is that by Christmas time
We'll be in Istanbul – though distant now it seems!
That is the city where Lord Lovat's Regiment
Plan soon to drink – their Victory Toast!

I end my song with blessings to each one of you;
And a hundred good wishes to Flora – my beautiful maid.
I live in hope that we shall soon meet and I promise her
One kiss will renew – our happiness.

ORAN A' CHOGAIDH

Deoch slàinte nan gillean tha Lòbhat a' sireadh
Deoch slàinte nan gillean tha linne 'san ám
Mo dhùrachd 'gan tilleadh gu sàbhailte rithist
Tha móran dhuibh bhuineas do dh'Uibhist nam beann.

Fhearaibh th'aig baile ri célidh nan taighean
Ri éisdeachd gach naidheachd mar thig as an Fhraing
'Gur garadh gu dòigheil mu theine math mònadh
gur mise bhiodh deònach bhith còmh' ribh 'an ám.

Chan ionnan is mise 's an corr de na gillean
Tha 'seasamh fo shileadh de dh'uisgeachan trom
Fo luaidhe nan Turcach is sligeannan miurt-te
Tha 'dòrtadh mar thuiltean gun sgur mu ar ceann.

Ged gheibhinn car tacain cead sineadh 'sa' phlaididh
Cha luaith' ni mi cadal cha tarruinn mi srann
'Nuair thig fios on Chòirneal a dhol ann an òrdugh
Gu seasamh an còmhrag 's a' chòmh-stri oirnn teann.

'Nuair thòischeas buaireas thig stoirm mu ar cluasan
Tha 'n talamhmun cuairt dhinn air ghluasad fo'r bonn
Bidh gillean gun ghruaman le'n gunna ri'n gualainn
A' leagadh nan uaibhreach 's a' bhuaidh bidh i linn

Bidh peileirean snaidhte mun cuairt oirnn am pailteas
A' fuaim a' dol seachad neo-thlachdmhor an srann
Bidh gillean bha tapaidh a' tuiteam gun fhacal
'S iad crioslacht' an acfhuinn gu batal nan lann.

Chan ionnan 's 'nuair b'òg mi a' siubhal le m'gheòlaidh
'S mo chompanach còir le'm bu deòin a bhith leam
Gunna geal bòidheach 's mo chù air an t-sòile
'Nuair dhèanainn-sa leònadh bhiodh Dòmhnall 'na dheann.

Ach sguiridh mi ghearain 's a chaoidh ann am earrann
Seasaidh mi daingheann gu cath a chur teann
Le Gàidheil a' chruadail 'sna blàir choisinn buaidh
Theid an Turcach a Sguabadh thar uachdar nam beann.

Thaar dòchas 's e daingheann mu laithean na Calluig
Gu ruig sinn Iostambuil ged is fhad' tha e thall
'Se 'm baile bheil dòchas aig Réisimeid Lòbhat
An dramachan òl 's iad victorious ann.

Mu sguir mi dhen òran mo bheannachd le deòin dhuibh
Ceud soiridh gu Flòraidh an òigh a tha grinn
Tha mis' ann an dòchas gur goirid gu'r còmhdhail
'S air m'fhacal bidh pòg ann 'toirt sòlas gu cuimhn'.

That's the one song of my father's that was written down. It was published in *The People's Journal*, Inverness, North Counties edition, 2nd September 1916. Later he composed a song about Glasgow, about a Uist man in Glasgow thinking of Uist, dreaming of home. My father was not what you call a dreamer, but he loved quiet; he loved nature and solitude. Here at home we used to fish out of Heisker each summer. We had a bothy, it was like a sheiling for us, and in the winter months I remember my father often talking about Heisker and about St Kilda. Everybody's heard of St Kilda but few people have heard of Heisker – it's the name of a small group of islands which are also called the Monach Islands. They lie seven miles offshore, west of Uist. Going out there in May and June, the place seemed like a paradise to the Grimsay fishermen; the *machair* would be a blaze of flowers. We'd go ashore from the boat, the cattle would be standing in the sun, the waters teeming with fish. My father had a great love for the old ways and the old people out there. He used to say he'd be happy to leave Grimsay and join them. But the population was going down and down. St Kilda was evacuated in 1930 and the last families left Heisker in 1943. That seemed to be that – but my father didn't want things to rest there.

For thousands of years Heisker supported small subsistence communities, usually in contact with the mainland of North Uist. A monastic settlement flourished there in the medieval period. The island had reasonable anchorages, 1,000 acres of fertile, well-drained ground, plenty of gamebirds, seabirds, shellfish, seals. So during 1943 and 1944, with another World War raging, my father was more and more thinking – 'Why should such a beautiful place be deserted?' And a plan to resettle the islands grew in his mind and when the war ended, in the autumn of 1945, my father took me and his whole family out to reclaim the island. I was twenty-two at the time.

When I was a boy, there were still eight families out on Heisker – big families. There was a school and there was the lighthouse. But by 1942 there were only two families left – two MacDonald brothers – and in that year the lighthouse was closed. Those MacDonalds had been there for generations. There were four or five boys in the one family and four or five girls in the other. That might have become a problem but it was the loss of the lighthouse that broke them. The lighthouse gave the Heisker people a feeling of security, and, of course, they got a small income as lighthouse attendants. In emergencies they would use the light to communicate with the mainland in Morse code. So it was that it was a critical poverty of numbers, which finally broke Heisker. And those last MacDonalds came away – one brother settled outside Fort William, one settled on Islay.

My father was close on fifty but he thought he could make a go of it; he wanted to reverse the trend of depopulation that was then at its height in all the Islands and Highlands of Scotland. He was a poet: with millions round the world killing each other for good and evil reasons, he had a vision of life as it might be, as it should be. And Heisker was a place where he felt people could live, be themselves and show the way.

I was born here on the island of Grimsay. It's a tidal island sandwiched between North Uist and Benbecula and it's now joined by a causeway to both. The land is deeply indented; rough crofting ground. My father was a crofter and like his father before him he was also a sea fisherman, so he knew the land was there on Heisker and he knew the land was good. He contacted North Uist Estate, which owned the island. His idea was to re-establish a properly viable, self-sufficient community. He hoped that at least five or six families would go from Grimsay to form a real, long-term settlement. Half a dozen showed interest but, one by one, they dropped out. My father, however, was determined – nothing would sway him – and in the autumn of 1945 we went out to Heisker. He believed others would follow when they saw us settled and prospering.

We left the house in Grimsay with just a bed, two chairs and a table. We let the croft to neighbours and we saw our going as no sacrifice – in Grimsay we had sixteen acres plus hill grazing, but on Heisker we would have 1,000 acres free range. It was a beautiful September that year. We sailed from Grimsay out over the Benbecula bar into day after day of blue Atlantic. We had an old lifeboat with a sail and oars and a petrol/paraffin six-horsepower engine. That transported all our goods and chattels. Almost a dozen journeys it took. My father had planned everything. Whilst fishing Heisker through the summer we had cut and dried enough hay for the winter, and planted potatoes. Nothing but the wild geese had grazed there for two years, so the grass was long and the rabbits had grown bold, but it seemed to us a land flowing with milk and honey.

Our rent to North Uist Estate was £25 a year. The agreement was that we had half the island but, of course, we had the run of the whole. There was no one else. We made arrangements to buy the best of the houses by instalments. There were six of us in the family, though only five went out because my eldest sister was just starting training as a nurse in Glasgow. There was my father, my mother Flora, my second sister (who was eighteen), my brother and myself. My sister was given special permission to be my brother's teacher. He was just twelve years old.

Our going out to Heisker was a big event in Grimsay. People thought we were crazy. Here we were, giving up comfortable lives to go to the

The Morrison family house, on the right, at Sandbank, Grimsay, c.1945. (LM)

unknown, to go back to the ways and a place that failed. You might describe our act as brave or foolish. But for us it was great. I would do it all over again. For my mother the years on Heisker were the happiest of her life. I remember coming back in the boat from the mainland and jumping down into the water. Turning round I saw my father looking out over the *machair*, with the sheep grazing and the cattle wandering back towards the byre and he said, 'Isn't this great? This is great.' I heard him say that. And the tears were on his cheeks. Being a bard and a storyteller he felt the poetry of the place and he enjoyed our defiance of the odds. The long nights out there forced him to keep the old stories alive, forced him to sing his own songs – there was nothing else. He had to be a bard; there was no school, no library-van, no radio. He hoped to form a kind of co-operative. He planned that those that were interested in the land would farm the land; those who were more interested in the sea would fish.

There was good pasture for hundreds of animals. Ourselves, we took out everything we had; three cows, a bull calf which grew to serve the cows, ducks and chickens. The bull stayed with us the three whole years; that was all right because all our heifers and the stirks went away to be sold at the North Uist cattle sales. We took out our own small flock of blackface sheep, and it was a good deal bigger when we came back. It wasn't the island, the animals, or the sea that undid us – it was just lack of people. Our family was too small to manage alone

Lachie Morrison (right) with brother and friends, c.1947. (LM)

for more than a few years. But that first winter was good. We felt so free on the island. I was making creels for lobsters. I was snaring rabbits and we were selling the skins, boating out thousands of skins. After two years without any predation or any competition from domestic animals, the rabbit population on the island had exploded. This would threaten our grazing and be bad for the crops we planted. We needed to kill them, but you could also make money out of rabbits in those days. I became a trapper, a skinner and a curer of skins. I would be getting thirty or forty a day, more. I'd skin them – I got very fast at it. I'd put a bunch of dried grass inside each skin and hang hundreds on nails. There were plenty of outbuildings with good roofs. The old houses with thatch were beginning to go, but I had what I called my 'drying station' – dozens of spaces for the curing of skins. I'd send them down to London in bundles of fourteen pounds weight, good air-dried skins. That was the maximum the post office would take – one stone. There'd be about a hundred skins in a bundle, depending on the weight of the skins. An older rabbit has a thicker and better pelt than a younger rabbit. Those were the skins you wanted. 'Best Wild' would fetch 2s. in London at that time, which wasn't bad. In calm weather in the wintertime we'd ship out a load

of fresh carcasses for eating, down to poulterers in the north of England. Rabbit meat was not despised in the 'forties. Rationing was still on.

My father was also fond of shooting. On the island he was always out with the gun. As a boy in Grimsay he used to shoot scart, cormorants. He used to go out with his best friend and he mentions this in his Salonika song. That friend was killed in France. They were both with the Camerons. My father never forgot him and when he was shooting, his friend was often in his mind. Scart, eider duck, mallard, barnacle geese, greylag, teal. All those my father would bring home. We were never short of meat. We had all the mutton we needed but we preferred the wild birds and a certain number of rabbits. That's what we lived on – wild birds and rabbits. We didn't trap otters, though there was still a market for otter skins in those days. But we did shoot seals for the oil. We rendered it down and it was mixed with grain to feed the cattle and sheep, and the chickens and ducks and geese we kept for eggs. It was very good feeding. We used to run it into lemonade bottles and take it across to the mainland. The crofters there would pay 3/6 a bottle. It made a valuable food supplement.

Seals were very plentiful and there were no laws against shooting

*The Lighthouse, Heisker, abandoned
1942. (LM)*

them then. Sometimes we shot from the boat and sometimes we shot from the shore. We skinned them, then stripped the blubber and cut it in cubes to be rendered down by a very slow heat in a cauldron. In fact, in the summertime, the heat of the sun would melt seal blubber. If you hung it up in old canvas, or a piece of muslin, the oil would drip through and it was so clear, perfectly clear. Like water-glass, with no taste, hardly any taste at all. It could be taken as a human medicine, like cod-liver oil. People on Uist would ask us 'Have you got any clear oil?' They would want it for sore throats and chesty coughs and things like that.

We didn't eat seal flesh. It tasted too strong of the oil for me. Later on I heard from a Norwegian that if you soaked the flesh in vinegar overnight that oil taste went – but I've never tried it again. The remnants of the seals would be fed to the dogs and the hens, but we made good use of the skins; we had plenty of seal skin rugs in the house. My father made handbags for my two sisters' going away to Glasgow. The fur of the young seals was best; it was longer, fully an inch. It was the young pelts that were used for fur coats and waistcoats. The pelt of an old seal would be damaged, with battle scars and years of clambering the rocks.

Before our time, in the age of sail, there was a big shipwreck on Heisker. The vessel was called the *Vanstable*. It had come from Dunkirk. Whether it was bound for this kingdom or was set to cross the Atlantic we'll never know, but in the afternoon of a wild winter's day, the *Vanstable* hit one of the many dangerous reefs around Heisker. The islanders rushed down to the shore to help. They could see the crew clinging to the rigging, but in such a sea nothing could be done. In the morning, when they returned, there was neither rigging, nor hull, nor sailors. It was as though the sinking had been a dream; but day by day the bodies came ashore and the islanders carried them and buried them out there on the west end of Heisker, opposite the lighthouse. The graves are there to this day.

Years ago there was a church at the east end of the island and there are graves around it, but in recent history no one was buried on the island of Heisker – the dead were always brought ashore to be buried in the graveyards of North Uist. The coffin would be taken by boat and most of the island would come with the body. A small flotilla under sail would cross the seven miles. There's one man up at Bay Head who still remembers that.

We always ate very well on the island. We'd bring flour in but we grew our own potatoes and vegetables. We could catch saith and laith at the mouth of the harbour, just a natural harbour. In the wintertime we'd go out in the small boat and pull them in, just as many as we needed. In the summer, going out to check our lobster creels in the lifeboat, we used to lay down baited lines – and pick them up coming back. We'd bring home baskets full of flounders, a few cod, garfish. We caught skate.

Lobsters we didn't eat; we sold them for cash. We stored them in square boxes and put them away by boat to the west side of Uist. There was a man there, Donald Mackintosh. He'd come down to the shore with his cart and take them by lorry to Lochmaddy and the steamer would take them to Mallaig. From there they went by train to Billingsgate. It was a long journey and in hot weather the losses could be very high – with nothing coming back here to us. Donald Mackintosh was a good man. He was born in Heisker himself and was related to the last MacDonalds who left in 1943. He was glad to help us; he was glad to see us out there on the island. We'd anchor offshore on a wee bit of chain and the provisions would be moved on or off, no bother. Donald had trained his horse to go out in the surf and that horse would back the cart out, right to the side of the boat. Sometimes the spray would be over his head.

Heisker is a flat island but a very beautiful island, a series of small islands connected by white tidal sands. In fact my father used to say Ceann Ear was like a big aircraft carrier and an ideal place for planes to land. He wrote trying to get some sort of service established, to try to take our lobsters out – but in those days, with all the problems following six years of war, nothing came of it. He was ahead of his time.

One thing that made our life enjoyable was the numbers of visitors

Piper Norman Johnson, of
Lochmaddy, on Heisker, 1997. (LM)

we had. Friends from Grimsay would come out to see us. It was an outing for them. Strangers came out. And every year a group of students came from Cambridge University – botanists. They were studying the flora of Heisker, comparing plants on the island with those on the mainland. It was the perfect place for botanists. The students were young men of my own age and we got on very well. Two of them still keep in touch right up to today. They fell in love with the island. They used to stay with us, but later, when the school came up for sale, those two students bought it and it's still theirs to this day. Their names are Richard West and Franklin Perry and they visited us here last year.

And so we lived our lives. And we did well. But no one came out to join us, not to settle. Most of the houses were still roofed – but no one came. When my older sister finished her training in Glasgow she came home to Heisker and my younger sister went off to replace her. So our number remained five for three years – which is both a long time and a very short time. Then we came away. It was in the autumn of 1948. We came back to Grimsay. My father settled back to mainland crofting as though he'd never been away. Though what he felt inside his heart will be another matter. He loved Uist but I think he loved Heisker more. This is his song, 'North Uist', written for the exiles in Glasgow, and elsewhere.

Come join me on the ferry to the island of delight
– Time will pass quickly going over the sea –
Visit beautiful places where everyone lingers
And welcome you'll be in every house in North Uist.

Your crops will grow well in the rich soil of the machair
Your cattle stand tall with fine calves in the fields,
Your sheep graze high on the summertime pasture –
Never will you fear destitution, nor your sheds lie empty.

Kelp drapes the rocks, the very waves carry fertiliser!
Fish in their plenty surround you – like the sea,
Life will be good – without hunger or cold,
Your peat so abundant – you'll never buy coal!

Shellfish from the shore you'll gather of all kinds.
If its rabbit you desire – to the sand dunes you go!
Wild duck swim in plenty on lochs full of trout
And on the wide open moorland you hear bellowing deer.

The folk you will find are kind and intelligent,
Honest and open in ways no money can buy:
Health blooms on the face of the young and the old
In the beloved island – the place of youth and my love.

No one could find a better place to spend eternity.
It's so different to walking the streets of the Lowlands
– Here you are safe and need fear no enemy,
Here you can sleep at peace in the shade of the mountains.

I am not the bard to praise the full extent of your beauty
(I would fail if I attempted to try)
But my blessings forever on both the place and the people,
For I've never seen better anywhere in the North.

The Morrison house, roofless and ruined, 1998. (LM)

So I offer my blessings to the island I praise
To all my relations – and those now sleeping forever…
It is my wish on the day my life will be ended
That I am laid in Clachan Sands in North Uist.

UIBIST A TUATH

Tuigainn leam thar an aisig do dh'eilein nam buadh
Chan fhairich thu fad'e 'dol tarsuinn a' chuain Séisd
Chì thu àiteachan maiseach far a math leat cur suas
Gheibh thu coibhneas 's gach dachaidh ann an Uibhist a Tuath.

Bidh do bharr air a' mhachair far an cinnich gach pòr
Bidh do chrodh ann am pàircean le 'n àl de laoigh òg'
Bidh do chaoirich air àrdain an raghainn an fheòir
Cha bhi éis ort gu bràch ann 's chan fhàilnich do stòr.

Gheibh thu òr far nan clachan, thig an todhar 'sa' stuaidh
Gheibh thu iasg ann am pailteas an taic ris a' chuan
Bidh gach nì dhut cho ceart 's cha tig acras no fuachd
Bidh do mhòine mu seach ort 's nach ceannaich thu gual.

Gheibh thu maorach 'sa' chladach far bheil iomadach gnè
Gheibh thu coinein 'sa' choilleig ma theid thu 'nan déidh
Gheibh thu lachainn air lochan 's bidh am bradan a' leum
'S ann a monaidhean farsuinn chluinn thu langan an fhéidh.

Chì thu sluagh gasd' agus taitneach 'nan dòigh
Gheibh thu aoigh agus ceartas nach ceannaicheadh òr
Chì thu ìomhaigh na slàint 'n aghaidh aois agus òig'
Ann an dùthaich mo ghràidh-sa rinn m'àrach o m'òig.

Cé 'n t-àite a b'fhearr dhut gu bràch fuireach ann
Chan ionnan 's mar thà thu an sràidean nan Gall
Cha bhi eagal romh nàmh ort bidh thu sàbhailt 's gach ám
Ni thu cadal gu sàmhach fo sgàile nam beann.

Chan eil mi 'na m'bhàrd chuireadh àird air gach buaidh
Cha deanainn ach fàilinn 'dol a sàs ann an duan
Bidh mo bheannachd gu bràch dhan an àite 's dhan t-sluagh
Chan fhaic mi nas àghmhor an cearn an Taobh Tuath.

Bheir mo bheannachd dhan àit' air am b'fhearr leam bhith 'luaidh
Far bheil móran dhe m'chàirdean tha pàirt dhiubh 'nan suain
B'e mo dhùrachd gach là 'nuair thig crìoch air mo chuairt
Mo chur sìnte 'sa'Chlachan ann an Uibhist a Tuath.

North Uist fishermen at their summer sheiling on Heisker, c.1960. Lachie Morrison is second on the right. (LM)

After leaving Heisker my parents did not return – not once – but for more than twenty years my brother and I spent every summer out there fishing for lobsters. The North Uist fishermen had always had their own little row of sheilings close to the shore on Heisker, where the boats were moored, and we went in with them. When the roofs were taken off, the whole lot of us stayed in the schoolhouse, with the permission of Mr West and Mr Perry. There were four smaller rooms and the classroom. So it made an ideal bothy and we had ten fishermen staying there most nights from April through to the start of September. I fished along with my brother until his eldest son joined him. Then they got their own boat, and I got a new partner. We'd come ashore of an evening after lifting and setting the creels and there'd be conversation and stories. Everything was Gaelic. Most of that generation could sing, not their own songs but the well-known Gaelic songs. Bachelor nights in the bothy. Great nights. And though few of us were natives to the island, things were much as they must always have been – save that there were no women with us, or children.

Not for one moment am I sorry we went. I was so glad to go. When you're young you're keen on everything. I loved the island. It was like a new world to me; it had a fantastic potential but, in the end, one family was not enough. How could it be? Each time my father and I went away to Uist we would worry about leaving my mother, my sister, my brother, alone. We might be cut off on the mainland for days and they would be marooned on the island. Nothing serious ever

happened but the doubt was there. Hauling boats was hard work for two men. My father didn't want to turn his children into hermits. So we came back. My sisters went away then and continued their nursing careers. My brother got married. Today just two of us are alive, my older sister and me. She lives here in the house next door. Everything's changed, the way it does. That's the way it's always been.

My father died in 1978, my mother six years before. He missed her a great deal, but neither regretted the step they took in risking their lives on Heisker. In their different ways both were proud of what they did, the hardship they endured, the joys they had on the island. Today, of course, life on Heisker would be a much easier option. So many things have improved – ship to shore radios, echo-sounders, every kind of electronic and satellite gadget. We had no means of communicating with land other than by manning our own boat. If it was a clear day you could signal trouble by lighting a big fire and making it smoke, but that was it. In bad weather there was no means of communication, perhaps for weeks on end. There were no subsidies for sheep or cattle, no grants for fencing. Everything had to be paid for on the nail in those days and we had very little cash. But there we were – and we were a lot better off the day we returned to Grimsay than the day we left. Not only in our pockets but in our hearts. My father was asserting the rights of the Gaelic people to land that had been theirs for thousands of years. It was courageous. Today Heisker is a nature reserve and maybe that is the best thing – but nobody lives there.

Lachie Morrison's Hebridean sheep stand about in front of the Morrison house, Sandbank, North Uist, 1999. It is now the headquarters of a thriving specialist wool centre., (TN)

When we left, it was the Cattle King of North Uist, MacAuley of Kirkibust, who took over the grazing. He knew he had something good – so much so that he made sure nobody saw what he had, or went out to the island at all! He made every building but the school uninhabitable. He took off the roofs. He knew the value of the Heisker grazings. He had a big boat, he had capital. He could take his animals out and bring them back to market just when he wanted. With money, he could run Heisker like a ranch, whereas we could only run it like poor crofters and it was always a struggle.

And so it came to pass that the Cattle King of Uist took over the Monachs and the Morrisons went away! But, in a way, you could say it was us gave him the island, because when we went out in the first place we offered to take some of his stock with us – for a herding fee – and MacAuley was pleased with the results. So, when he knew we were leaving the island he negotiated his own deal with the North Uist Estate and took over. He didn't go out there to live. He didn't send a stockman out – he just sent out young animals and brought them back full grown. And economically that was the right thing to do – the summer grazing is first-rate and the winter grass is as good as any in Scotland. With the Gulf Stream all round you there's often enough no frost at all. MacAuley was master of his situation and we were pawns in God's great plan! A big, fourteen-hundred-weight beast could cause no end of trouble in a small boat like ours but MacAuley could ship a dozen three-year-old stirks no bother. And he made a big success of it. And good for him. But, looking back, the sad thing is we could have done what he did; we could have farmed Heisker from the west coast of Uist. Even from Grimsay we could have done it. Because in taking the island we acquired rights to two 'holding crofts' on the west side of Uist. Those were the crofts that had for generations served Heisker, holding the stock that was going out or coming back. We could have built houses there and run Heisker from Uist, which is, of course, more or less what MacAuley did. But there you are, we were thinking like crofters, not thinking like landowners or ranchers. And my father's dream was settlement, not money – so here we are in Grimsay. MacAuley worked away for years but when his son took over things went down hill and fell apart. Now Heisker's been sold to Scottish Natural Heritage. It's a nature reserve though one of the fishermen winters a few sheep there still.

I was fishing out of Grimsay until my father died and then I took over the croft. When I reached retirement age I thought my hopes of marriage were over. Then I met Theona. I'd been content all my days. But something changed and here we are. I met a beautiful woman. At the age of sixty-nine I got married and at seventy I became a father to a wee boy named Patrick, after my father. He's a splendid little chap. We count our blessings. I hope to be around for him a good number of years yet. He's speaking good Gaelic and we're hoping the

Lachie Morrison with his son Patrick on the shore, North Uist, 1998. (LM)

Lachie and Theona Morrison with
their baby, Patrick, 1996. (LM)

gift my father had has skipped a generation and come down to him.

And we've started a new business, or rather Theona has started a new business with a friend from Edinburgh, Dorothy Hogg. They're making and selling woollens made with pure Hebridean wool. We've got Blackface sheep and Cheviot cross Blackface, but we've moved sideways to specialise in the Hebridean sheep. It's one of the rare breeds. They're small and light and easy to handle. They seem to be very intelligent. They flock well. They're black-brown and they're horned. Some people confuse them with the St Kildan. But there are big differences, noticeably that the Hebridean flocks whereas the St Kildans don't flock, they scatter. Evolution is a wonderful thing. The Hebridean is brave like the Musk ox. If the Hebrideans see a stray dog they flock together on the highest knoll or hill and they stand at bay to defend themselves. The meat is very tasty and the wool is a fine, soft wool. We run the business by mail order.

It all began about ten years ago. The crofters had, for years, always sold all their fleeces to the Scottish Wool Board. But the Board unfortunately has no interest in Hebridean fleeces. They are of no economic value to them – they are just a nuisance to them. So we had to think of something to do with them. We enquired about getting the wool spun and woven by women in the community here, in the traditional way, selling the product as special and traditional. It was very difficult to organise. Then we met Donald Montgomery. He's a Lewis man who's managing director of Johnstons in Elgin. They're one of the great wool companies and we're pleased to say he took us on. We now work in harness with Johnstons. We produce and buy in Hebridean wool and they turn it into high quality, very fashionable blankets, jumpers and scarfs. Then we sell them by mail order. Its' beginning to take off and it brings interesting work to Grimsay. Employment remains a problem here, as it is all over the islands. We don't want Grimsay to go the way of Heisker.

One day on the island I'll never forget. It concerns a man who came to Uist from Vancouver in Canada. He came out to Heisker with one of the fishermen from the mainland of North Uist, and he asked to be put ashore on Ceann Ear, the west island, where he'd been born and brought up. His old house was a ruin by then, no one having lived in it for years, but he asked the fisherman to leave him and he made camp at the good gable end. He'd left the island more than sixty years before, at the age of nineteen. His name was MacDonald.

He then went down again to the shore where he found an old creel and he baited it with shellfish and he set the creel off the rocks where he'd fished as a boy. Then he went back to the house and he slept by his old fireplace under the stars, and in the morning he went down to his creel. And there was this fine big lobster inside, waiting for him. He went back, made a fire and he cooked it and ate it. Then, when the tide went out, he made for the ford to the middle island, called Shuinich, and crossed to the east island where the fishermen had told him we were living. And he stayed with us then for the best part of a week. He talked about his life on the island, the people he knew when he was young; about Heisker in the 1870s and 1880s, when there were well over 100 people on the island. He still remembered the old songs. He told us about his life in Canada. With the Second World War he thought he would never see Uist again, but peace came and in 1947 he crossed Canada by train and sailed back to Britain.

Well, the day came for him to leave Heisker and my father asked me to ferry him back to Uist. It was a dull, grey day; the sea was calm but there was a deep swell running. We had the sail up and I was at the oars, rowing. He was in the back of the boat and I was looking at him as he looked back at the island. Suddenly it seemed appropriate that I should sing and what came into my mind was not a Uist song but 'The Lewis Boat Song'. And as I sang, the tears were rolling down from his eyes. Everything was so real – the words of the song were painting a picture of the very event we were a part of. For nineteen years Heisker had been his home and his life. Now he was an old man, in his eighties, knowing he would never set eyes on that island again. It was though you were saying goodbye to someone you have loved all your life. He had made a good living in Canada, but could never forget the island of his birth nor the days of his youth. It was an inspired choice I made and I think neither of us will forget that day as we two sailed, a young man and an old man, from Heisker to Uist.

THE EVERLASTING SWELL —
A BOATING SONG OF THE MEN OF LEWIS,
Domhnaull MacIomnhair

The everlasting swell —
Hear the sound of the high riding waves,
The sound of the sea
That I heard as a child;
Unchanging and pitiless
They mix the sands of the shore —
The everlasting swell,
Hear the sound of the high riding waves.

Great wave after wave
Races forward to whiteness,
Surging and rolling
And irresistibly breaking;
Yet, one by one, their momentum
Ebbs and dies on the shore —
And so died each soul
That once lived in this village.

It was never in the woods
Of the west I sought comfort,
My longing and thoughts are shaped
By the sands of the sheltering bay —
Where all those so generous
In spirit, friendship and happiness,
Lie exposed in the open —
Like the roe deer that flees from the mouth of the hound.

I once knew this place
as joy dancing with life —
And young people were gentle
And kind in their nature,
And good wives were content
With the love of their husband,
And the sheep and the boar
At their doors in the morning.

Now willows and rushes
Choke the clear springs
Where often I quenched
The wild thirst of my youth:
The cold ruined homes
Are now ragwort and dock
And brown nettles stand
Where the hearth was so warm.

But now I must leave you
and we'll never meet again –
My days here are numbered,
For age has made itself plain:
So, when I am wrapped
In the cold slumber of death,
Make my bed there' –
By the high-riding waves.

AN ATAIREACHD ÀRD

An ataireachd bhuan,
Cluinn fuaim na h-ataireachd àrd,
Tha torunn a' chuain,
Mar chualas leam-s' e 'n am phàisd,
Gun mhuthadh gun truas,
A' sluaisreadh gainneimh na tràgh'd,
An ataireachd bhuan,
Cluinn fuaim na h-ataireachd àrd.

Gach làd le a stuadh,
Cho luaisgeach, farumach, bàn,
'N a chabhaig gu cruaidh,
'S e gruamach, dosrach, gun sgàth,
Ach striochdaidh a luath 's
Aig bruaich na h-uidhe bh' aig càch,
Mar chaochail an sluagh
Bha uair 's a' bhaile-sa tàmh.

'S na coilltean a siar
Cha'n iarrainn fuireach gu bràth,
Bha m' inntinn 's mo mhiann,
A riamh air lagan a' bhàigh
Ach iadsan bha fial
An gniomh, an caidreamh, 's an àgh,
Air sgapadh gun dion
Mar thriallas ealtainn roimh nàmh.

Seileach, 'us luachair,
Cluaran, muran, 'us stàrr,
Air tachdadh nam fuaran
'N d'fhuair mi iomadh deoch-phàit'
Na tobhtaichean fuar
Le bualan, 's cuiseag gu'm bàrr,
'S an eanntagach ruadh,
Fàs suas 's a' chagailt 'bha blàth.

Ach chunnaic mis' uair,
'M bu chuannar baethail an t-àit'
Le òigridh gun ghruaim
Bha uasal modhail 'n an càil,
Le màthraichean shuairc,
Làn uaill 'n an còmpanaich gràidh
Le caoraich 'us buar,
Air ghluas'd moch mhaduinn nan tràth.

Ach siubhlaidh mi uat;
Cha ghluais mi tuilleadh 'n ad dhàil:
Tha m' aois 'us mo shnuadh
'Toirt luaidh air giorrad mo là,
An àm dhomh bhi suaint';
Am fuachd 's an cadal a' bhàis,
Mo leabaidh dean suas
Ri fuaim na h-ataireachd àrd.

Lachie Morrison (right) digging peats, North Uist, c.1950. Beinn Eaval is in the background. (LM)

Mina MacKay Stevens

EILEAN NAN ROAN, SUTHERLAND

'The very fish were killed by the force of the waves, they were thrown up onto the shore in their thousands.'

I was a mischievous child and my greatest desire when I leave this world is to see again my grand-uncle Angus. I do hope I will see him. One of the things I liked to do when I was a girl was to turn on the tap and watch the water trickling out of the boiler, shining against the darkness. Many a hammering I got for that! And afterwards I used to race to my grand-uncle and he would put his arms around me and shelter me, like this. 'Fágaibh am páisd marbh sibh!' he would say, 'Leave the child lest you kill her.' He suffered in his last years from asthma and I would go up to his bedroom and open the window wide and fan the air across him as he sat in the bed. He kept pan-drops on a trunk beside him and he would say in Gaelic, 'Gabh fhéin fear on bhodachan body …' 'Take one for yourself – take one from the old man.' And I would take one and give one to him and we would sit talking together. I had such a liking for that old man. It's unbelievable.

I was born in 1912, but the first thing I remember clearly was the Armistice of 11th November, 1918, and the great bonfire we burned. Most of the island boats had been laid up through the war, and the old ones were thick-coated with tar, so all the elderly men – they were the only men left on the island – and everyone able to wield an axe or hammer, went down to the shore to break up those boats. And we carried the broken boards in creels and bags on our shoulders up to the top of the small hill behind our house and stacked it in a pyramid. It stood on the high point of the island. And that fire burned gloriously. I can see it now – and everyone was cheering – and slowly we saw the other fires being lighted – at Melness, at Tongue, at Brae Tongue, at Scullamy and Straithie Point, along the whole north coast of Sutherland. And I can still hear my auntie saying, 'Mina, don't you think our fire is the best!'

Eilean nan Roan, Sutherland. A storm photographed by a cameraman sent by The Daily Record, *1937. (DR/SK)*

That same auntie made me a beautiful kilt to start school. She had gathered the wool; she had teased and spun it, she had woven the cloth, dyed it with green lichen she had collected from the rocks and she gave it to me. But as soon as I sat at my desk on that first morning, I got intrigued by the ink-well! The china was so white and the ink so black in the hole. I put my finger deep in the well and out shot the ink! All over me and my new kilt. Little things like that stick in my mind. Carrying my peat to school for the fire; the register sitting there on the front desk; eight names being called; the strap hanging ready; dusting the blackboard and taking the cloth home to be washed; scrubbing clean the floors and the desks; spinning our massive wooden globe of the world; in wintertime the yellow light of the paraffin lamps; running home so happy to be free. There were no names or numbers to any of the nine inhabited houses on Eilean nan Roan. Everyone was related – everyone knew everybody – so there was no need to start labelling where we lived. MacDonald the Post was in charge of the boat and he knew the island like the psalms – by heart.

Looking back, it was the First World War that ensured the decline of Eilean nan Roan. My father and fourteen of the younger island men served away in the Navy, and through the winter of 1918–19 they came home. One man served in the Air Force and two in the Army, of whom one was killed. Coming home, father was content enough, but the younger men could see no future on the island. The fishing industry collapsed. There was nothing to do. Emigration was the way out. From one house three sons and one daughter went away to Australia. Others went to Canada and the United States. When they got settled and got houses, the sons would send home for their parents. The families that went first were those that depended on the sea. The families that stayed had crofts, but things were hard for them, too, and with the young ones away the old and infirm were unable to cope. On 6th December 1938, on a dark and stormy day, my father and the last eleven islanders left the island for ever.

The history of Eilean nan Roan remains very obscure. John George MacKay, who wrote a booklet called 'The Story of Island Roan', says that the island was first settled in 1820, in his grandfather's day, by families evicted from Strathnaver and Borgie in the Sutherland Clearances. That's what all the families on the island believed – but their belief was not fact. I've recently been reading in the *Country of Strathnaver* that in 1726 there were four families living on Island Roan. And in 1799, Sir John Sinclair's Statistical Account also states that there were four families – thirty-six people – on Eilean nan Roan.

It's therefore clear that Eilean nan Roan was inhabited long before the Clearance period and there must be something more to the story than folk memory suggests. Either the original inhabitants were removed to make way for the newcomers, or the newcomers joined the original inhabitants. Or the original population continued a natural expansion in marriage contact with the mainland. Certainly the population of Skerray and the whole seaboard of Sutherland increased hugely between 1810 and 1830. In the census of 1841 the population of Eilean nan Roan is recorded as comprising seven families – every one a MacKay – forty-two people in total. In 1881 there were seventy-eight people, all MacKays but for one big family of MacDonalds.

I left the island to work on the mainland in 1927, but my parents, Donald MacKay and Jessie Anderson, stayed on till the end in 1938. Everybody was related but nobody knew who their grandparents were.

Where did the island people come from? For years I have tried to find out, and I've got nowhere. Nobody of my generation from Eilean nan Roan knew who their great-grandparents were, or their great-great-grandparents. Or if they did, they kept quiet about it. My mother's mother lived till she was eighty-seven but she never spoke of her parents. Why was that? Maybe they were a little backward in their style of dress; maybe they were very poor; maybe she was adopted, or felt some shame attached to the family. We just don't know what our

The great cave at the back of Eilean nan Roan. (DR)

people were before they went to the island. But maybe they weren't cleared to Eilean nan Roan; maybe our people were living on the island long before people can directly remember. I've heard a rumour that one family was moved over for stealing potatoes, but if that was true, that family was transformed by the island, because in our day everyone on Eilean nan Roan trusted each other like brother and sister and they shared what they had like a mother and child.

As a girl I had a good life on the island. Of course we knew nothing different. The island people were very thrifty. They lived more or less self-sufficient, any money they made they hung onto. This was a prime reason why, after three generations, the islanders had the money that gave them freedom to leave and set up on the mainland or emigrate abroad.

Eilean nan Roan is one mile long by three-quarters wide. It's a treeless and windswept plateau of fertile land above high cliffs, with one small landing place and almost perpendicular steps. We had plenty of fish, hens, eggs, milk, butter, cheese, good vegetables. The cattle and sheep were quality beasts. We had drying winds and the hay stored well right through the winter. We put layers of salt between each layer of hay. The island is part of the Duke of Sutherland's estate. It had a quarry which produced excellent building stone. Everything had to be carried by hand, but our houses were well-built stone houses with good slate roofs.

Gales we would have but very little ice or lying snow. The grass grew for a good six months. Our milking cows were tethered or herded by the boys. The sheep were free. But you had to watch them. They'd be sitting on the green in front of the house on a hot summer's day and they'd be chewing away. Then all of a sudden they'd rise; one, then another and another and they'd wander down along a path from which they never deviated to the shore, and out to graze on the rocks where grass or seaweed grew. Now that was all right; they knew the falling of the tide and we knew the tide was falling. I remember asking my grandfather, 'How do the sheep know when to rise and go down to the shore?' And he said, 'There's something below their toes that tells them when the tide is going out.' I don't think he was joking and there's no doubt that those sheep were gifted with a sense that told them when the tide was dropping in their favour. But they had no sense as to when the tide was rising! No sense of when their rocks were about to be cut off from the shore. That's why they had to be watched. And from the age of five to the age of fifteen I was a shepherdess. That was one of a hundred jobs I had.

I remember one March I was told to keep a special watch because the big springtides were flowing. The great springtide of the birds. I was out on the Mount Shore at the back of the island. I saw there was going to be trouble, so I ran back to get my aunt Kirstie whose sheep were mingled with ours. The men were out at the creels. I remember the panic she was in as we ran side by side along the cliff. The sheep were hungry and heavy with lambs. We tried to call them in but they didn't come. We had to go out and try to drive them off the rocks but the tide was rushing into the gullies behind us, cutting us off. The sheep scattered and were jumping rock to rock – but one ewe lost her footing and went down into the sea. She was going to drown, so I jumped in beside her. The waves were coming over the both of us and she was getting heavier and heavier but I was determined – and I kept her head up and kept pulling and shoving till at last her feet found a ledge and she got clear of the water. Then she just sat down, exhausted. The other sheep were all wandering up the path to the top but she gave up the ghost, she lay with the waves crashing onto her. At last, Auntie Kirstie came down and between us we got her safe to the top. Then she took off! We went home soaked to the skin.

Each summer the islanders would take their cows across to the mainland and up on the hill to the sheiling at Airigh. Most families had two cows. One cow would calve in the spring, for milk through the summer, and one would calve in the autumn, to give milk through the winter. My grandmother used to go across with her next door neighbour, Cardie. They had been going across since they were girls and they walked the cows on the hills this side of Tongue. Every year they looked forward to going to the sheiling and I used to go over and join them during the summer holidays. The women of four families would be gathered there at the sheiling. The only man would be my grandfather. After the day they would all come out to sit on the hill and enjoy the evening. The women would sing and we children would join in the choruses. The bell heather would be out and the road winding below us. One car a day might pass, or a wagon, and the sun would be right round to the north over the sea. We had a polled blue-grey called Kate and a horned red – she was called Boyan. She wasn't a boy but we called her Boyan.

When the old ladies were milking they usually sang. Everything on the island was Gaelic, except for our schooling. The singing soothed the cows and allowed the milk to flow. The old women would make cheese. We had one problem, up there: sometimes we had very little good running water. It was difficult to keep the buckets and jugs and pots clean. We used grit from the burn for scouring. But back on the island we had plenty of water and dishcloths and drying towels. Not far from the house my mother had a huge iron pot set in a small stone wall. A fire was lighted underneath to heat the water. The towels were boiled in water and soda, and we had big bars of soap. Everything was dried on the bleaching green. On the hill, washing was dried on the whine bushes. It was sterilised by the light of the sun and came in beautifully clean – pots as well.

We had no problem with bacteria in those days. Things were primitive but, as far as I can remember, the doctor only came to the island twice in the fifteen years before I came away to work. People from Eilean nan Roan occasionally went across to the doctor's surgery up in Tongue, but in those days the waiting room was always empty! Not like today. The first visit by a doctor concerned my uncle, Hughie MacKay. He had gone to the mainland and was coming home from across the hill towards the shore. It was very hot and he got thirsty and he drank running water from a burn. He knelt down by a rock where the burn ran clear and cupped his hands like this. Then he pushed off his boat and rowed back to the island. That evening he told my aunt, 'I'm not feeling well,' and as the night went on he started to hiccup. He began to vomit and by morning he was very ill. Four of the island men took a boat the five miles to Tongue, climbed up to the surgery and brought the doctor back to the island. There was no speech on that boat, not a word was said. The doctor was known as a silent man. He belonged to Lerwick and his name was Dr J. V. Irvine. He examined my uncle and decided he must have drunk infected water or poison. He ordered that Hughie eat nothing and drink nothing, not even a spoonful of water. And a district nurse was sent over to the island to oversee his treatment. Even when he begged and cried out for water, he was given nothing.

At last he started to get better and my auntie was asked to boil a fresh chicken. Just in water with a little salt. No barley, no peas, no greens, no carrots. Well, my uncle Hughie sipped this broth and he said it was wonderful and he felt much better. And he asked if he might have a wee bit of the breast of the chicken. He seemed so well that the nurse cut him two small pieces and gave them to him on a willow pattern plate. Twenty minutes later he was very ill and within half an hour he was dead. When the doctor heard of this, he was livid with anger. He said the nurse should never have disobeyed his orders. After he'd signed the death certificate, he said he thought the water must have trickled down past a dead animal that had died on the hill.

The second visit by a doctor to Eilean nan Roan concerned my second cousin, Jimmy MacKay. He was proprietor of the Scrabster Hotel in Caithness. He used to send drink out to the island. Say you wanted a bottle of whisky, or a bottle of port for Christmas or Hogmanay, Jimmy would send it down to Skerray and across it would come, by boat. Nobody was to worry about payment – but in May, when the weather was good, Jimmy would come down the coast collecting the money. It was like a holiday for him. He'd be taking a drink here and there and taking new orders. Well, one May he came over to the island and I remember him calling round to our house and saying to my mother, 'I'd love to have some of your girdle scones and a glass of milk from old Kate.' She was the blue-grey. That night my father went next door and stayed up late with Jimmy and his brother, Angus. They were talking about the old days on the island and it went on very late. My father came home but the two brothers, Angus and Jimmy, slept in the same room. When Angus awoke, he got up and came across to our house, but he didn't notice Jimmy was dead. It was my Auntie Kirstie, when she took him up a cup of tea, who looked at him and touched him and realised he was dead. It was a shock for everyone. Coming down for breakfast that morning, we children immediately realised something was wrong. I remember leaning over the banister and seeing that my father had his boots on the wrong feet, at ten to two. Everybody was silent. Dr Irvine came to certify the death. He told us that he'd already rung through to Scrabster and the doctor there had told him that Jimmy had a heart condition. He'd had a bad heart for years, so there was no need for a post mortem.

But things didn't finish there; a great storm blew up and raged for days and days. No coffin could be delivered, nor the body taken from the island. In the end the lifeboat came up from Scrabster with a coffin. It was still too rough for a landing, so the men went out to meet the lifeboat and they brought the coffin ashore and up to the house, where the women had dressed the remains. In those days it was always the women folk who dressed the remains. The men then carried the coffin back and down the steps to the jetty and rowed out into the gale, four men on the oars and two holding the coffin. It was the lifeboat took Jimmy's body way back to Scrabster.

Dr J. V. Irvine was a wonderful doctor. He never lost a confinement in his life. But he did have one weakness: he was not a dentist and he had no patience with bad teeth. If you had a bad tooth on the island you just had to put up with it. The only cure we had was a small bag of salt pressed hard against the gum or a large glass of whisky swirled round in the mouth. If things were really bad people went over to Tongue to see Dr Irvine. His cure was 'Pull them out!' No injection, no gas – he just pulled out any tooth you complained about and given the chance he pulled the lot!

One day, when I was seventeen, working at the Kyle Hotel, I went up to see him about a persistent toothache. He looked in my mouth, gave a grunt, rummaged about in his bag and brought out what looked like a dirty pair of pliers. He nearly took the head off me! I was in such pain that I turned at the door and said, 'Dr Irvine, I'm never coming back to you again!'

'So be it,' he said, 'but I think you'll need me before I need you.' And he ushered me out. Of course, what he said was true.

Well, I didn't want to ever face another experience like that, so the very next week I got a lift to Inverness to see a proper dentist, to get all my teeth removed. Once and for all. I'd heard that this Inverness man used injections. He told me I had eighteen teeth. He said he'd take out nine that day and nine the next day, which was thoughtful, but I told him my lift that afternoon was the only way of getting back to Tongue for a week, so I opened my mouth and he took out the lot, there and then. No – first he gave me a large toddy! Then the injections. Afterwards I sat in the waiting room for half an hour, then made my way to the car. Inverness to the Kyle of Tongue was a poor single-track road in those days. Bump, bump, bump the whole way. We got back to the hotel at half past two in the morning. I started work at seven-thirty and I was on duty all day. What a head I had! But I think my mother had it even worse. She had eighteen teeth out at the herring fishing. No injection, no cocaine and straight back to the gutting, her face looking pretty much like the bench she was working!

The church on the island was the schoolhouse and the schoolhouse was the church. My grand-uncle Angus was the senior elder and he took the services. He was the one who gave me the pandrops. The precentor was Colin Mackay. He had a fantastic voice and when he was giving out the line it was wonderful to hear. He used to play draughts with my grand-uncle and I used to stand at their shoulders watching. At home we had prayers and readings from the Bible everyday, grace before and after every meal. We didn't sing the psalms in our house but we were close enough to hear Colin singing up in his house, such a strong voice he had. The Psalms of David. When I read them today, I hear Colin's voice as it was on the island.

In all my life I don't think there will have been a day when I have not heard or read the word of God. Every morning at home, we read from the

Children from Eilean nan Roan school, photographed on a visit to the mainland, early 1930s. (SC)

Bible after breakfast and before we set off for school. Then when we got to school we started the day with prayers and more Bible readings. If I was late the teacher always knew why! My father would continue to the end of the chapter, always read the psalm complete. Christian Old Testament religion was deeply ingrained into everything we did on Eilean nan Roan. Everyone strove to be upright and immune to the trials of the flesh with us. The day of the death of a man or woman was 'written'; it was there to be met like the tide.

I still say grace and I still say my prayers morning and evening. I pray for my family, the ones that I know, and for the government, the ones that are in it now. I'm hoping they'll do very well.

I remember one occasion when there was a disturbance in church. My cousin Willie had asked me 'Have you got any peas? Dried peas.' And, of course, we had plenty. Every year we dried the pods and split them open and stored the peas in jars in the kitchen or in the blackstone pantry outside. 'Bring some', he said, 'to the church tonight!' I put several handfuls in my coat pocket and during the service, when William couldn't stand the proceedings any longer, I felt him put his hand in my pocket to take hold of the peas. He was going to fire them from a pea-shooter he'd made – but things never got that far. I must have put too many in, for, as he withdrew his hand passed the flap of my pocket, the

peas started spilling! They ran everywhere! Tap-tapping and jumping! What a noise! My cousin, Hector, was sitting down by the blackboard. He burst into giggles, most of us did — we couldn't help it! Then a terrified silence fell on all the children and on the whole congregation. The service continued, but afterwards, what a dressing down I got from my father and grandfather and Auntie Kirstie, for desecrating the Lord's House. It was me that got the blame — for taking the peas from the pantry without permission. I remember that like yesterday. And still my grand-uncle Angus loved me.

All the church services on the island were in Gaelic. The only time there was English used on Eilean nan Roan was during Sunday School and in the school, and sometimes when visitors arrived. My first teacher had Gaelic but the second one didn't; she was against it. One hundred lines, copyright, was the punishment for going back into Gaelic. All our schooling was in English, but it was necessary for us to learn English and we were taught very well.

We never had modern type ceilidhs on the island, but I used to play the accordion. I would sit on a big round stone outside our house. It had a hole in the centre. Somebody's taken that stone away from the island now, but for me it was like a magic stone and whenever I sat down to play, our next door neighbour would come to his door, dancing, and then come up and dance and dance round me whilst I played. That was John, my father's first cousin. That would be on summer evenings after we'd had our tea. High teas we had; our dinner we ate in the middle of the day. How he would dance, old John MacKay! Many an evening he must have sat there waiting for me — to come out with the accordion. And I would often creep out very quietly, trying to make sure he didn't see me, or hear me, until I was on the stone. Then I would play. And out he would come. He was a beautiful dancer.

Because of the First World War and my father being away, I was six-and-a-half years old when my next sister was born. I was very much 'the older child', and therefore had to look after all the younger ones as they came on stream. I had to do all the donkey-work and lugging about. When I was thirteen my mother went away to hospital and I was left in charge of everyone — my father, grandfather, my brother John, baby Donald, who was six months, my sisters Nan and Chris. It wore you down, so, by the time I was fifteen, I was desperate to get away and to work on my own. I was baiting lines, mending nets, making nets and helping my father make creels. I was put in charge of the garden before I reached the age of ten. I liked that. My aunt used to send me packets of seeds from the mainland. We had beautiful leeks, plenty of carrots, parsley. There was kale for the sheep and cabbages for us. We spread herring nets to keep the birds away. We had plenty of rhubarb. Also, the lady in Tongue House used to give the women of the island permission to go across to her house in the season to pick

John MacKay, aged 89, oldest inhabitant of Eilean nan Roan at the time of the evacuation. It was John who liked to dance whilst Mina MacKay practised her accordian.
(DR)

blackcurrants, gooseberries, raspberries. 'Not the strawberries and no apples!' The strawberries were eaten in the dining room and the apples ripened too late for us, but we got plenty of the others and brought them back for my mother to make jam.

I grew potatoes and turnips. We had Golden Wonders for the back end. We had Kerr's Pinks for meats and we had Champion potatoes to go with the herring. They were stored in a clamp. On a good dry day they'd be laid on the dried bracken and covered with bracken like thatch. It was cut with a sickle at the back of the island. Coming back with the sheep of an evening, I'd carry it down in a creel or bundle. This bracken thatch was then covered with divots, grass turf, cut at the same time as the peat. The men would skim the turfs with a flat spade and stack them to dry in the wind, like peats. Last, the divots would be covered with earth and sand: a good clamp would keep out ice, frost and rain for a year. We cooked potatoes in a big bean pan. The salt went in when they came to the boil. If the potatoes were young they were cooked in their skins; if the shoots were appearing we'd break them off and put the tubers in a bucket of cold water, overnight. That firmed them up if they tended towards the soft. I still do that for myself.

All the ploughing was done with the *casdirach* or the *cas chrom*, the old hand plough. We had no horses and no tractors. Our harrows were made of wood. The rope went round your shoulders and you just pulled the harrow up and down, then across, then up and down again. It was my grandfather who broadcast the corn, walking and casting in a steady rhythm. Then we harrowed the ground again, to bury the seed out of sight of the birds. On the island of Strona they had bullocks for ploughing – that took the drudgery out of their lives. Strona is a much bigger island than Eilean nan Roan, but Strona only lasted nine years longer than we did. It was evacuated in 1947, after the very cold winter.

Drills were made for the potatoes and planted in dulse – that's what we call seaweed. The dulse was gathered on the shore and carried in creels on our backs to the field. Dulse was for us both soil and fertiliser. And it fed both the sheep and ourselves. We planted carrots for the sheep as winter feed. The cows never got carrots because they flavoured the milk. Nobody cares about that kind of thing these days, they feed cattle meat! But in our day you knew what the cows were eating by how the milk tasted.

The last job each evening was counting and folding and feeding the sheep. Around the walls of the fold, on wooden pegs, bundles of food would be hung. Hay or carrots or grass. We didn't use dogs for the sheep or the cattle. There was only one dog on the island. A dog was more trouble than it was worth. Dogs might drive the sheep off the rocks into the sea or over a precipice. The only dog on Eilean nan Roan belonged to the MacDonalds – two brothers – the

boatmen. Their grandparents had come in from Durness.

We ate very little butcher meat. Each house killed two sheep and they were salted and kept over the wintertime. A butcher would come over from Tongue in the autumn to do the killing. The meat was stored in a barrel. The poor cuts would be used for soups and the best meat for main courses. We ate plenty of eggs but no bacon – except when we were tilling the ground and harvesting. That was hard work and the bacon came in from Thurso. We had plenty of cockerels. They were our usual fresh meat. They were Sunday dinner, reheated because of the Sabbath.

Nothing was wasted. We had to be economical with everything. We churned our own butter. It was put in big earthenware jars and covered with bees' wax to keep the butter sealed and airtight. That was women's work and the children took their turn.

We poured melted butter over our potatoes and fish – that was the main course each day. We kept jars of salted crowdie, some plain and some with caraway seeds. We bought sugar, and kept tins of milk for emergencies. We were

John Mackay playing draughts with Donald John and Chrissie MacKay, 1937. (DR)

heavy on tea and we all drank it with milk and sugar. Tea was one thing we'd run out of – but the neighbours would share one with another.

We took great pride in our house. It was not a small house – we had three bedrooms upstairs. We had a sitting room and a big kitchen, a small washroom and another bedroom. On a Saturday morning I would take out all the chairs from the kitchen and scrub them down. Our rugs were sheepskins, dyed; not with natural dyes but commercial dyes sent up from London. My mother had two aunties who lived in London and they sent us dyes – brown and red were the two main colours.

Our kitchen had a large modern stove, a really big stove, which one of the aunties got for us. She had worked as a cook, for a doctor and his wife, and when she got married this stove was her wedding present. It couldn't have been suitable for her in London, so it was sent up to Wick, from Leith, on a boat and then on to the island. It was a beautiful stove with a boiler at the end of it, and big hood. You could cook girdle scones, oatcakes and pancakes; boil a kettle; simmer, fry, oven roast; everything. The other houses had open fires and a big kettle hanging on a chain from an iron hook.

Each summer we used to take our hen-house up to the back of the island well away from the garden and the corn. And near this henhouse was a small mound that always stayed green, even when everything round it was scorched by the sun. We children were told that a pot of gold was buried there in the ancient days. But others said it was treasure buried by a pirate who lived on the island and sailed the coast in a ship painted red on one side and white on the other, so that nobody knew who he was! But whatever was said, or believed, no one ever dug or despoiled the green hill. The thought never entered our heads. In Gaelic the story was that the treasure lay where the rays of sunrise and sunset met.

There are two large caves on the island, which we called 'the Day Cave' and 'the Night Cave'. Both were at the back of the island and you had to go by boat if you wanted to get into them. My father told us that once someone put a dog into the night cave, by boat. It was not seen for days. Finally the dog reappeared on the other side of the island – without a hair on its body! The cave must have got very narrow, or that dog must have suffered a shock of some kind! Recently I heard a poem by Sorley MacLean called 'The Cave of Gold'. It's a long poem but bits of it remind me of the story of the hairless dog of Eilean nan Roan. It's about a piper entering a cave, wishing he had a third hand with which to fight off the great dog attacking him. The dog which he calls the green bitch of death.

> A cry from the cave itself,
> The pipes shouting his farewell,
> While the young goats and calves
> Were loud and uncaring on the ridge.

There was superstition on Eilean nan Roan. I heard it said that after Babsie MacKay's family moved off the island, they believed they had been cursed. One of the boys got ill and didn't get better. So they effected a cure by bathing the child in gold and silver. They put the boy in a bath with their gold rings and all the silver they could find in the house and washed him. And he was cured. It was a *buiteach*, said to have been put upon the family by the mother of Willie John Mackay, after one of them married a mainlander. A *buiteach* is a threat, a *buitseach* is a witch.

We didn't eat scart or wild birds of any kind. People on the mainland used to eat mackerel but we never ate mackerel. We had haddock and herring in season. All the lobsters caught on the island were sold away, packed in dulse and carried in creels to the post office in Skerray. From there they were put in boxes and on the bus to Thurso. Then down to Billingsgate by train. It was a long journey and the lobsters had to be alive when they arrived or you got paid nothing. Often enough we would get a ticket back saying 'twelve dead, twenty-three dead, forty-one dead', and the live prices were not high to the fishermen.

We didn't fish for crabs but we would eat crab claws if they happened to be caught. We also ate whelks from the rock pools. A lot of fish was salted. My father built himself a smoker at the end of the barn. The oak chips he used came down from Orkney. He mostly smoked haddock, finnan haddock – we took the bone out. In the summer months he supplied the hotels, the hunting lodges and the fishing lodges right down to Altnaharra. Local people wouldn't buy fish – they didn't have the money or they caught their own – but the hotels were part of a buyer's market. Considering the labour that went into smoking and salting and the quality of the fish they were getting, the prices we got were very low. It's amazing the weight the base of the pyramid takes for the glory of those on the pinnacle. And it's me now that complains, not us then.

Every family had to send people away to make their living. My mother followed the herring fleet right down to Yarmouth. Until my father got his own boat, he went away every summer to fish out of Peterhead. He sometimes brought good money home and coming back he would always bring the best cured herring. He'd been with his firm so long he was allowed to choose his own herring. They were perfect. They arrived in boxes, coming home to the island by train, by bus, by cart and by boat. Packed twice, they would be soaked in brine, taken out and salted again. Some years the skipper of the herring boat would call in at Eilean nan Roan to drop my father off at the end of the season. When I was about thirteen, I remember standing down on the steps to welcome him home and the skipper stopping my father with one hand on his arm and saying, 'She's going to be a sizer! She's going to be like Queen Elizabeth!' After that I never grew another inch! There was great comradeship on the boats.

Hector MacKay taking student David Hammond out to Eilean nan Roan, c.1970. (SC)

Our own best haddock came from the Mackway island, where the tides are strong. These were the fish we chose to salt. All would be line caught, not netted. They were gutted and washed, and you had to see there was no blood left in the bone. Then they were tied in couples and put in wooden tubs and salted and left for one night in the brine. Next day you took them out by the tail and put them in a basket, for carrying up to the '*yeos*' at the back of the island. A *yeo* is a place where the rocks overhang a sea inlet, and where wooden poles were set between the rocks. The salted couples were hung on these poles and at each flood tide the waves would fling their spray up over the fish. And so they hung in the clean air of the Atlantic for five or six weeks – douched twice a day by the tide. No sunlight fell on the fish. The gullies were deep, clean and covered with ferns. Both cattle and sheep would be kept back from the *yeos*. Those haddock ended up solid and dry but not stiff like the salt fish you buy today – the quality and the taste of the sea-cave salt fish was superb. They were finally stored in barrels and would last all winter and more. To cook them, you cut them in two, took out the bone and fried them in butter.

The Eilean nan Roan boat crossing to Skerry, c.1930. (BM)

We did not fish for salmon. The islanders had no rights to fish for salmon. Every summer plenty would gather around the mouths of the Borgie and the Naver rivers – but they were watched by the bailiffs night and day. It was against the law to net salmon from a boat. Sometimes you couldn't help catching one or two – but the men didn't throw the dead ones away! One day I remember hearing the children shouting 'Salmon!' and running down to the harbour to see the men standing up surrounded by sixteen huge, monstrous salmon they'd brought back from Dalness. What a sight that was, but in minutes they disappeared – shared round amongst the families. We had two good spring-wells on the island. Beautiful water. They never went dry but a lot of carrying had to be done in pails.

The postman rowed across twice a week from Skerray with the mail. That was in the summertime. And he might bring or take messages. Later on it was a big improvement for us when my father got a motorboat, built up at Eribol, with a Kelvin engine. You can imagine the years of saving that went into a purchase like that, like buying a house today – but all the money saved beforehand. The boat made everything easier and my father took that boat over to Skerray when we left Eilean nan Roan. It was lost the night the *Princess Victoria*

went down on the Irish crossing, going out from Stranraer, January 1953. The very fish were killed by the waves – they were thrown up onto the shore in their thousands. My father's boat was matchwood. The other island boat was lost that same night, battered to shreds. On the island, if the men saw a storm brewing the boats were always taken up on the shore. Here on the mainland, not depending for their lives on the boats, a slackness set in.

Everything was well organised on the island. There were never any disputes. There were just a few simple rules which people accepted, and different people were the authority on this or that. Donald MacDonald the Post was in charge of the boat that ferried people over to Skerray. If he said, 'We're not going over to the mainland today, because it's going to blow,' that was it. Nobody would argue and say, 'But we must go!' There was no disharmony. One depended on another; a balance was struck and a natural authority accepted. On the boat it was always the two MacDonalds on the rudder, time about. Wonderful characters and very good seamen. Their grandmother, old Betty MacDonald, came to the island as a young woman and she never left it – except to be buried. Nobody was buried on the island. She was hardy and crusty and like nobody else. She was the only one on the island who I saw stand up to the Duchess of Sutherland.

Many people speak against the duke and duchess but the people on Eilean nan Roan were well treated. The Sutherlands helped two of our families get settled in Skerray. I know they gave great help to MacDonald the Weaver. He injured his leg in a fall when young and became a cripple. He could only walk with crutches. So, the Sutherlands twice sent him to hospital in Edinburgh for treatment, then to Golspie, where he was taught the weaver's trade.

Every summer the duchess would come up the coast in the yacht *Catania*, anchor off shore and come in on the steam pinnace. One year the pinnace went aground on shallow rocks covered in dulse. Because it was summer there were only women, children and old men on the island, so the women went out to refloat the pinnace – they were highly skilled oarsmen. The duchess rewarded the success of their mission with dresses for every woman on the island. A tailor was sent over, each woman was measured and each chose the pattern and material they wanted. The dresses lasted for years and then got remodelled into kilts for the children.

The *Catania* was a beautiful ship with a streamlined clipper bow, yellow funnel and black hull. All the upper structure was painted white. The boys, especially, loved to see her. And sometimes they were allowed on deck. There are 2,000 names in the visitor's book Duchess Millicent gave the islanders in 1883. We children liked visitors coming over. It made a change and the boys would be selling them blown bird eggs gathered on the cliffs for cash. They'd put all the different eggs on cotton wool, all measured out from big to small. Two boys were killed in falls from the cliffs.

One day the duchess decided to visit each house on the island on the lookout for pieces of antique crockery. She was offering prices. When she got to Betty MacDonald's house, she met her match. Not that Betty knew the price of anything – but she wasn't the woman to be asset-stripped. As the duchess went round lifting this and that, she'd be saying in Gaelic, 'Well, she's not going to get that! And she's not going to get that either!' And so on. And the duchess was asking, 'What is she saying?' Of course, in the end, the duchess did get a few things and you might say the honours were shared. Probably it was the few very valuable things she took – like the knockers today.

Although all the men on Eilean nan Roan worked the sea and most of the women made regular crossings to Skerray, no one from the island ever drowned from a boat – not in living memory. There were many near misses because no one on the island could swim and the waters are cold – but that's as it was. We all had great respect for the sea and I, myself, always had a love of the sea. I remember one Saturday going across to Skerray to get the messages and do various jobs. We got the boat well filled with stores – sacks of flour, sacks of oatmeal and oil-cake for the cows. My father was standing on the quay with

MacDonald the Post and the time of our return had come. All the crew were ready to sail but one woman was missing. Johan MacKay, an older woman married to a man on the island, and she was pregnant. I remember the Post saying 'The wind's going to blow! It's just waiting for an airt to blow from. We'll not make it back if we wait for her!' But just at that moment we saw her, at the top of the hill, coming down from her sister-in-law's house. We could see her coming and she could see us – she was trying to hurry. So we waited. Her hurrying seemed so slow. We should have left her but we waited. The minutes passed and the wind was rising.

At last Johan arrived and she climbed into the boat and we cast off. As soon as we got out of the harbour we got hit by a tremendous shower of snow. It was like getting slammed in the face by a door. Before you could count ten we were lost in a sheer white sheet of fury, a blizzard! It whipped the sea into a roaring torrent of waves, the snow and spray was lashing our faces! We couldn't get back into the harbour, so we had to go on. The seas were coming right into the boat. There were four men on the oars but they could do next to nothing in a blow like that. The woman who was the cause of the trouble had fainted. She was sprawled in the bottom of the boat – out for the count – but nobody paid attention to her. The Post and John MacKay were on the rudder, my father and the crew were on the oars. I remember my father shouting, 'Bail water, throw the

Hughie Campbell MacKay and Chrissie MacKay feeding chickens outside their crofthouse, Eilean nan Roan, 1937. (DR)

sacks over board!' I was just seven and clung on for dear life. By sheer luck we drifted into the shelter of the island. The men made headway on the oars and we got into the steps. Stepping ashore my father said, 'I thank the Lord that we are saved. Never in my life was I out in a sea like that!' Prayers were said as we stood in the boat. Everything was lost but our lives. I remember Johan being helped up the steps, trembling with cold, and going away up to her house.

But it's a strange thing, I wasn't frightened – I think I enjoyed it. And the next Saturday I was keen to go over again. I have no fear of the sea and one of my grandsons is the same. I can see it yet, every wave coming right over the boat, the voices of the men, the hands of the men on the oars. The only kind of water I'm frightened of is still water overhung with trees; deep pools in a river where weeping willows trail their leaves into the surface of dark water. That has frightened me. You don't know where you are – it's that, not the sea, makes me think of drowning.

The harbour on Eileen nan Roan is called Port na Coinnle, 'the Harbour of the Candles'. Some say it's called that because of the brightness of the water there on moonlit nights. Some say it was because we had to place lamps or torches on the cut steps to light the boats in, if they came home at night. But the real reason for the name goes back to a shipwreck in the nineteenth century. The SS *Onega* was returning from Montreal to Dundee. Whilst trying to shelter behind Eilean nan Roan, in a great storm, she foundered off Coldbackie sands. The whole crew was lost. The bodies of three men were seen afloat off Eilean nan Roan and brought ashore and laid out above the high-water line by the small harbour. Each body was covered with a tarpaulin sail. Next day the islanders planned to take them to the mainland for burial. During the night another storm arose and two of the men went down to the harbour to see that the bodies were safe and the tarpaulins secure, and there they stopped, for around each body glowing lines of white light flickered and shone in the darkness. Each tarpaulin was surrounded by candles burning, despite the wind and spray. The two men stood in silent awe. The one said a prayer, and they went forward together. And there they saw that the rings of white light came from the sea phosphorous draining from the bodies, the hair, the clothes of the sailors. It was a sight that neither man would ever forget, and after they'd told the other islanders, the harbour became known as Port na Coinnle.

My mother, Jessie Anderson, was born on the mainland at Clashaidy overlooking Eilean nan Roan, and she had a special reason to remember Port na Coinnle. She married my father in Thurso, then bride and bridegroom were brought home to Eilean nan Roan under sail from Scrabster in a fishing boat. They arrived to a great welcome from everyone on the island and more from the mainland. As they climbed the almost perpendicular steps the

men fired their guns in formal salute. Then, singing and dancing in procession, the whole company moved up to *am bail* where a great feast was set out in the open. After that the music and dancing went on till morning. That was 1911.

   I did quite well at the school but I wasn't able to go to High School in Golspie. I qualified but, as soon as I was old enough, I had to go away to work, to bring money in for those back at home. And when I left I only returned once in the eleven years before the evacuation, and that was for two nights only. I was fifteen and I went away to work in the hotels. My father gave me his New Testament. He'd carried it with him all through the First World War. He served on the mine-sweepers. 'I ask you', he said, 'to read this each night before you go to bed, no matter how tired you are.' Some times I was so tired I could only read one verse. But I did what he said, and I still do. That was our up-bringing. We were the Free Church, the Wee Frees.

   My first job was in Bettyhill Hotel and my only worry was where would I get the money for a uniform and shoes. The price was twenty-five shillings, for the material. That was the selling price of twenty-five lambs! I

Above left.
Sutherland Highlanders of the
First World War. Alexander MacKay
of Eilean nan Roan on the left,
c.1916. (BM)

Above right.
Christina Ross MacKay,
Howdie midwife and bonesetter
in North Sutherland, c.1890.
Chrissie was grandmother to
Babsie MacKay. (BM)

John George MacKay, author of the booklet 'The Story of Eilean nan Roan', with his wife Johan, daughter Babsie and sons Charlie and Ian, c.1924.

remember asking my mother where I would get those twenty-five shillings. I'd worked at home for years but in those days no child expected payment. Today children expect money and there's no word about giving, or work. My mother gave me the money and it was my auntie who made the uniform up. A blessing would always be said for one going away down the steps.

After Bettyhill I was three years in the Tongue Hotel, then I worked for Sir Robert and Lady Blank in Thurso Castle, then I was down in Troon. I was a waitress and head waitress. I started at fifteen shillings a week. The food was bad and the work was hard. You started at half-past six and you worked on till nine at night. In 1940 I got married and I've now lived here in John O' Groats for sixty years. I would have liked to have gone south but my husband didn't want that. He was born in the old part of this house and we stayed. He had a transport business.

My father and mother left Eilean nan Roan in 1938 and the other ten inhabitants came away with them. The *Daily Record* newspaper sent a photographer to record the end of island life. Most people settled locally on the mainland. My father and mother went to a place called Torrisdale and he bought a house from a woman. It was just a few miles away from the island. It didn't cost much because this woman was a widow and she was going to be sent into what was termed the Poor House and my father didn't want her to have to leave her old home. So he said to her, 'You can stay in the house, in the sitting room end, as long as you live and share with us,' and they made an arrangement. Her name was Jeannie Mackay. Now the roof of that house was painted tin but it wasn't lined, there was no sacking. And the house was small, so I worked with my father and my husband-to-be and we dressed the lot with second-hand wood. And we built a new kitchen, sitting room-cum-bedroom, a bedroom and a bathroom. It became a very nice house.

That house lies under a hill called Jane's Brae and there's a short cut over the top to a place called The Dam, a wintering place for the tinkers. One night in December there was heavy snow and wind and it was about ten at night when there came a loud knocking on the door. It was my mother who opened the door and there was a young man, with behind him a young woman, and in her arms she held a new-born baby. It was only a day old. And he asked if could stay the night in the barn because their tent was blown with snow. So my mother took them into the house and gave them tea and whatever she had. And they bathed the bairn in front of the fire and they dried him in a towel. Then she got our old army blankets down and took that little family out into the barn. It was clean and warm, with good hay stacked to go around them. And they slept there the night and went away in the morning telling my mother that she had saved the life of the child.

The mainland, for us, was more full of strange events than the island. Late one Saturday night my uncles George and Donald went down to the harbour at Skerray, to haul the boat up. There was a full moon and they rowed the boat to the shore but when they started to haul they noticed this black cat sitting at the back of the boat. My uncle Donald flung a stone at the cat but it was never away. Stones were going right through that cat but still it stood. Suddenly they realised that it wasn't a proper cat, not a natural cat, and one fellow said to the other, 'That cat is the very devil himself.' You see it was already Sunday morning and them still at work.

Another night my mother was coming home from Sculaby, over the hill through the heather. When she came to the smithy, a black dog rose beside her and walked close enough to be touching her leg. As she tried to push it away she suddenly realised none of it's paws were touching the ground. That smithy was an eerie place and some would say an evil place. One Saturday, the Saturday before the sacraments, the two sons of the smith were there, and a cousin of ours, Bob Murray, and another fellow, a stranger. Bob Murray was a good fiddler and that night he played for the others to sing round the anvil. Later they sat down to play cards, the four of them. Drink was passed round. Well, the game went on for some time until Bob Murray happened to look under the table and he saw that

Eilean nan Roan from the air, c.1990. (IF)

stranger had neither boots nor feet — but horses hooves! He suddenly realised who the man was. And, at that, Bob Murray put his cards on the table, rose from his stool and went to the anvil — where he broke his violin to smithereens on the iron! Then he threw the pieces, with dangling strings, into the forge and left the smith — without speaking a word. He went away and turned to be a minister and a very good minister at that. It was only later that he told anyone what he saw that night. That happened just before I left the island, so it must have been about 1925.

Another time my mother was coming down from Strachan when she found herself so hemmed in by a jam of people that she could not walk. She stopped — but there were no people there. She was alone and she knew she was alone, but when she started to walk, once more she felt the crowd jostling round her. The confusion stayed with her until she came to the burn and crossed

running water. That night in the village a child died. What she had encountered was the funeral procession. I have never witnessed such phenomena myself, though my son Iain, back in the 'fifties when he was a teenager, witnessed something similar. He used to go fishing out from Skerray and walk the three miles up to my mother's house. Now, there is a churchyard about a quarter of a mile from the house and, as he approached this, he saw a great circle of light appear in the sky. Orange it was, with a white outer ring. It got brighter and brighter and when he got to the graveyard it seemed to hover straight over his head. Suddenly he became afraid and he ran for his life. When at last he had the courage to look round, the light was gone – the whole place was in darkness. Like Eilean nan Roan out there in the sea.

Donald MacDonald

TARBET, LOCH NEVIS

'*Last week a man came by on* The Western Isles, *seeking the throne of Scotland.*'

It's four hours over the hill from here and twelve miles by boat to Mallaig. A four-hour walk or a four-hour row — that's how it used to be in the old days here. There's still no road but now it's just half an hour by a fast motor boat. I'm the last of the Loch Nevis people, on this side. There's Cameron Mackintosh, the impresario, and two or three of his people — but since my sister Jessie died, there's just me. We were the last of the old people. I have a pet lamb, she was born here. And she'll die here, like me. We're more cut off than most of the islanders — so, if I'm going in this book, I hope you'll put me in with them, with the Lords of the Isles.

When I was young there were plenty of people on Loch Nevis; crofters, fishermen. The tinkers would walk in from Morar to sell their things — tin, pails for the milk. There was a market for them — so that tells it's own story. There's nothing for the tinkers now. There was a lot of fishing in Loch Nevis. Before the railway, Tarbet was a bigger place than Mallaig. This was always a great loch for herring. But Mallaig came up and this place died down.

I was the youngest of the family. I was born in 1915. My mother and my father had a blackhouse and a croft about a mile from here at Ardintigh. That's where I was when I was a boy. It was later on they moved up here to this house at Tarbet and it was here that they died. Ardintigh was burned to the ground. Fishermen they think it was, staying overnight. They must have left something burning. It's just tin sheds there now. This house is a big house. It used to be an inn, long ago, at the time of the fishing. This was the place where they landed the herring. All the salting and barreling went on here at Tarbet. They came in here for a drink and some would stay over night. The bay here was full

Opposite.
Donald MacDonald of Tarbet, Loch
Nevis, 1998. (TN)

Donald MacDonald at the door of his house, Tarbet, 1998. (TN)

of skiffs and they'd go round to Loch Hourn. Loch Nevis and Loch Hourn were great places for herring, but Loch Nevis has more shelter from the wind. In Gaelic, Loch Nevis means 'The Loch of Paradise', Loch Hourn means 'The Loch of Old Hornie', the Devil. Whether this was because of the wind, the currents, the people who lived there, or some other reason, I don't know, but often enough there'd be a wind in Loch Hourn. The Tarbet boats would go out to the Skye lochs and they'd come back full of fish from Loch Scavaig, Loch Slappin, Loch Eishort. But after the railway came up from Fort William the herring boats went straight into Mallaig and all the salting and barreling was done down there, and there was nothing coming in here. The number of boats got less and less. Ring net fishing it was, they used to sweep them round the shoals of herring. Now its all purse nets they use out of Mallaig.

This house was the pub and one day there was a man came in from Campbeltown. He didn't know the loch and he got stuck on a bank near the mouth of the harbour, here at Tarbet. Now this bank was known as An Cailliach, 'The Old Woman'. And he was stuck there for several days. And the Tarbet people were talking about this, about the man from Loch Fynne who got stuck on the cilliach. They were talking about this in the bar when the very man walked in the door. As soon as the woman at the bar realised this was the man from Loch Fyne she asked him, 'Was it you, the old man, got stuck on An Cailliach?'

'No, no, no – it wasnae me,' said the man, 'I havnae put my old man in a woman since I left Campbeltown and I never got stuck all the length of my days!'

Because the herring is a silver fish and a plump fish, people think they must be a young fish – but herring can live to a good age. You wouldn't think that to look at them. The age of the fish can be judged by the size of the scales and the scale growth is proportionate to the length of the fish. Maybe that's where they got the word scale from, I don't know. Some herring live to be twenty-five, and that's one reason why the population fluctuates so much. Some years are good years for breeding, and some years are bad, but the effect of an exceptionally good year will last twenty years – because they live so long. I was born in the great years of the herring boom.

There's a book about the sea, written by two men, Russell and Yonge, which tells you about the fluctuations in the population of herring in the North Sea and the Minch. It was 1904 that was the great year for the spawning of herring. That was a miraculous year and they were still catching those herring in 1924. The peak years for landings were 1910 to 1914, the year before I was born – the year the Great War broke out. Those war years gave the fish shoals a rest and that was a good thing because, with the steam-drifters coming in, fish stocks would have gone down much quicker than they did – but for the war and the great spawning of 1904. Thousands of millions of fish. In 1919 the catches of white fish suddenly increased as well and that proved that restrictions on fish can be a big benefit. In fact the fishermen here have told me they caught many more thin and undernourished fish at that time – which shows that the grounds had become overcrowded and that proves the need for a balance between nature and man's intervention. Of course, nature will look after itself – that's nature – but what man does needs to be done with some thought, not just of the day but for the future.

My father was Donald MacDonald to name, like myself. My mother was a MacRae from the head of Loch Nevis, but originally her people came in from Kintail. They had eight of a family. Now I am the last man, the last man in Tarbet. My father's people were always here on the Tarbet side but his mother came from Ardnamurach – that's about three miles east from here – they were Gillies to name. It was a mixture of things we did; crofting, fishing, stalking. It was the Lovat family from Beauly had the estate in my father's time. They had Knoydart too. John MacKay was the last of the old people over there, now there's only incomers.

It was in Knoydart they had the last of the Land Raids. That was in 1948. The number of crofters was going down and down and the men who'd come back from the war made a claim for land, for themselves and their families. They got help from Father Colin MacPherson. The owner was Lord Brocket; a great admirer of Hitler he was, in the 'thirties. Most of his family took a spell in prison. They had no feelings for the rights of the Knoydart men or their families. They were being forced into exile. So, it was on Tuesday 9th November that the

Donald MacDonald's house stands beyond the old inn at Tarbet, part of the Cameron Mackintosh estate, 1998. (TN)

Knoydart men staked out sixty-five acres of arable ground. It was not very much, but the weight of the law came down against them and in the end they lost the case. But it was a big story all over Scotland and a man named Hamish Henderson wrote a song about it.

> 'Twas down by the farm of Scottas
> Lord Brocket walked one day,
> And he saw a sight that worried him
> Far more than he could say –
> For the seven men of Knoydart
> Were doing what they'd planned:
> They had staked their claims and were digging their drains
> On Brocket's 'Private Land!'
>
> 'You bloody reds,' Lord Brocket yelled
> 'Wot's this you're doin' 'ere?
> It doesn't pay, as you'll find today
> To insult an English peer!
> You're only Scottish half wits!
> But I'll make you understand –
> You Highland swine, these hills are mine!
> This is all Lord Brocket's land.

'I'll write to Arthur Woodburn's boys
And they will let you know
That the sacred rights of property
Will never be laid low;
With your stakes and tapes I'll make you traipse
From Knoydart to the Rand.
You can dig for gold till you're stiff and cold
But not on this 'ere land!'

Then up spake the men of Knoydart –
'You shut your f—ing trap!
For threats from an English brewer's boy
We just don't give a rap.
For we are all ex-servicemen,
We fought against the Hun –
We can tell our enemies by now –
And Brocket you are one!'

When he heard these words that noble peer
Turned purple in the face.
He said, 'These Scottish savages
Are Britain's black disgrace.
It may be true that I've let some few
Thousand acres go to pot,
But each one I'd give to a London spiv,
Before any Goddam Scot!'

'You've a crowd of Tartan Bolshies!
But I'll soon have you licked.
I'll write to the Court of Session,
For an Interim Interdict.
I'll write to my London lawyers,
And they will understand.'
'Och to Hell with your London lawyers,
We want our Highland Land.'

Above left.
Donald MacDonald aged seven, with
his father Donald MacDonald and
his eldest brother, Sandy, 1922 (all
smoking). (DM)

Above right.
Sandy MacDonald, 1929. (DM)

When Brocket heard these fightin' words,
He fell down in a swoon,
But they splashed his jowl with uisge,
And he woke up mighty soon,
And he moaned, 'These Dukes of Sutherland
Were right about the Scot.
If I had my way I'd start today,
And clear the whole damn lot!'

'You may scream and yell, Lord Brocket –
You may rave and stamp and shout!
But the lamp we've lit in Knoydart
Will never now go out.
For Scotland's on the march, my boys –
We think it won't be long:
Roll on the day, when the Knoydart way
Is Scotland's Battle Song!'

That was fifty years ago. That man, Arthur Woodburn, was Home Secretary in Clement Attlee's government. But just last week Cameron Mackintosh signed a contract to help the local residents in Knoydart buy the whole estate. How it'll work

out we don't know. Cameron Mackintosh has been very good to us here. It was his auntie's house he bought. It's not a big place that he has, though he's done it up very nice. Not a big house, but he's got 15,000 acres of land, mostly mountain.

The school here was up at Kylemorar. We used to walk over the hill. The building's there yet. There were three families living on each side of Kylesmorar and there were three keepers' children coming in from further up Loch Nevis and from Kinlochmorar too. There would usually be six or eight or ten of us in the school. All English it was. Difficult at first but soon we were used to it and we'd switch between the two languages just like that. All my brothers and sisters went away to work but I stayed on the croft. When my parents died my sister, Jessie Ann, came home. She was not married.

Three cows we had and three followers. The ground is very steep here for cattle; it was sheep was the law here. We had plenty of sheep. We'd drive them out to Morar and put them on the train to Fort William. Later on it was cheaper to send them out by float, diesel lorry. We took the rough with the smooth. We grew a few oats for the cows. Hay. Potatoes. There was a time when we had more cattle herds and in the summer they'd be taken up to the sheilings – but that was before my time. Tarbet is a bad place for sun. We lose it mid October and we don't see it again till the end of February. Knoydart gets the sun all day, but not us. We're round the bend!

We used to get the basking sharks in here, in the late summertime.

I remember Gavin Maxwell very well. *A Ring of Bright Water* — that was the title of his book about the otter. He used to come in here when he had the shark fishing station. There was a man from Texas with him. It was later on that he went in for otters. We have dolphins, porpoises, whales — 'sea pigs' we call them. Everybody had to know the sea in those days.

Before the railway came in, people always went up to Broadford on Skye to get their things, their messages, the bigger things they needed. Broadford was a good day's sail. And sometimes they'd sail right round to Fort William. But in my day it was just the twelve miles to Mallaig. We had a small skiff with a sail in the herring days, but when I was a boy it was just a rowing boat we had. It was my father did most of the rowing. But sometimes coming back from Mallaig in the evening, we'd stick up a small sail if the wind was in our favour, and my father might sing us home as the twilight came in. He used to sing 'The Song of the Deer' and the song of the man who went to Canada.

Last of all we had an outboard motor and, of course, sometimes we'd use the postboat, *The Western Isles*. The post office here was originally up at Kylemorar but the man died and it was my brother took the post over and he brought it down to Tarbet. He was postman for many years, and then it was me. I was postman here for forty years. When I retired they sent me a certificate. The boat would come in about three o'clock and we'd try to deliver everything the same day, at least in summertime. We'd go right up to the head of Loch Morar; we had a rowing boat moored there, especially for the post. Rowing was easier than walking the shore. But if the weather was rough we had to walk anyway. We'd go up to Ardnamurach, down to Stoul. It was exercise.

The Tarbet church was built in 1885, a Catholic church. That was the heyday of fishing. The people here were always Catholics, from way back. The priest would walk over from Morar once a month, or come by pony. That was the way horses would come in, with packs. The track was better in those days because it was used. Later on the priest came in by boat from Inverie — that's on the Knoydart side. Everyone would gather in. There was a family down at Stoul — they came up for the services here. And sometimes we would go across to Inverie by boat for services there. On Christmas Eve we'd go to Morar for midnight mass. By boat we'd go, we'd be away all night.

The old graveyard was at the head of Loch Nevis, on a tidal island. There is another on the south side of Loch Morar. They're not used any more. It was eighteen years ago they closed the church. There were too few people. Now it's been changed into a hostel for the backpackers. There's a man, Frank Conway, looks after it. He was a coal miner down in Fife. Since he was a boy he loved the hills, he was always a mountain walker and climber, so he's pleased to be here. 'It's my swansong,' he says. He comes over to ceilidh with me. The years go by so

Previous page.
Donald MacDonald's sister, Mary MacDonald, Tarbet, 1930s. (DM)

quick. We had ceilidhs here when I was young. We walked out with a lantern with a candle inside. It was a cup of tea by the fire – and if someone had been out to Morar or Mallaig, they'd tell us what was going on. A dram would be served at Christmas time, not other times. Small things I remember. Before bed we used to say our prayers. My father would carry me on his back. I remember sliding down his back to the floor, so clearly. And it seemed a long way.

We get tourists in here, and plenty of backpackers from all over. Last week a man came by on *The Western Isles*, seeking the throne of Scotland! 'The man who would be king', the boatmen called him! He was an American – Frank W. Maurer! Back on his mother's side he's a MacAlpine and he claims direct descendant from the wife of Kenneth MacAlpine, first King of Scots. He says he's a Pict. He's been touring his kingdom in a hired Ford Escort, sleeping rough like Prince Charlie! In a plaid. He's just awaiting the call. He won't ask to be paid, he says he just wants to represent the people and play his part in the rebirth of the nation. He's a big man and he looks good. He runs a quail farm and Wilderness Conservation Centre twenty minutes north of Davis, California. He's fifty-eight, but he told the men he plans to live to be 120 and reign for sixty years. I think he will have a claim, but so do five million others! As a MacDonald, I claim no more than allegiance to the Lord of the Isles.

Above left.
Donald MacDonald with the old
Catholic church, now a bunk-house
for backpackers, Tarbet, 1998. (TN)

Above right.
Frank Conway, warden of the
backpackers' hostel, Tarbet, 1998.
Donald MacDonald's house is
in the background. (TN)

Top.
Dyeing the tweed, 1936. (NM)

Bottom.
View from The Western Isles,
sailing north down Loch Nevis
towards the Isle of Skye and the
Cuillin mountains. (TN)

Opposite top.
Frank Maurer, 'King of Scotland',
aboard The Western Isles,
1998. (TN)

Opposite bottom.
Donald MacDonald, the last man,
Tarbet, Loch Nevis, 1998. (TN)

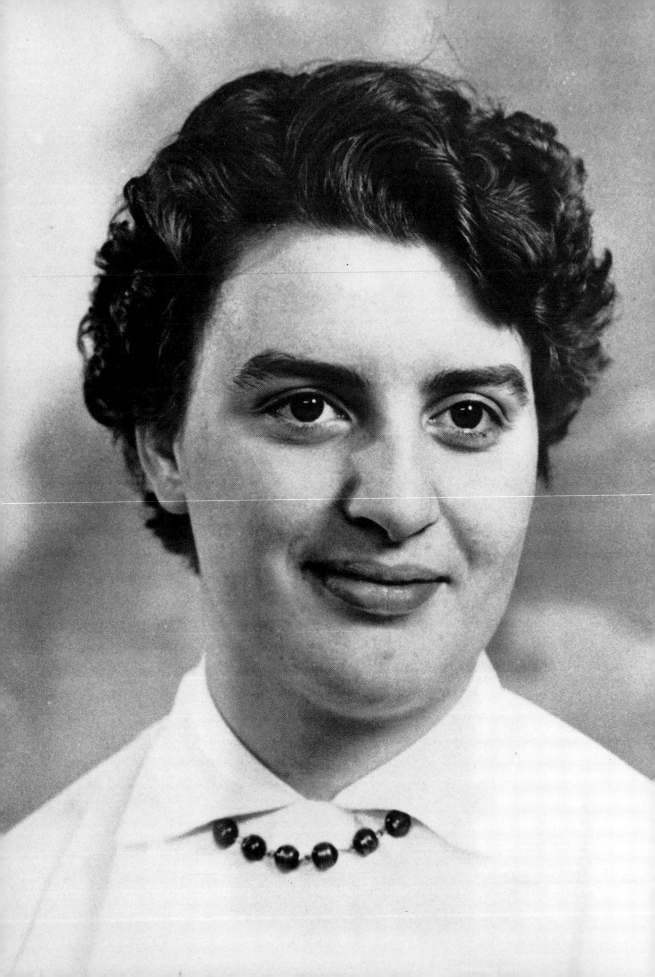

Margaret Dennison

PAPA STRONSAY, ORKNEY

'I used to watch them going up for their ice cream at Stackaback, singing.'

Opposite.
Margaret Dennison of Papa Stronsay,
c.1970. (MD)

My father's people came down from Fair Isle. That's about fifty miles north of Stronsay here – and you can still see it on a good day. There's a story that a man working on Stronsay saw a reflection in the clouds of a man ploughing with a horse on Fair Isle, close-up and crystal clear. It must have been the product of freak weather conditions, something to do with refracted rays – like the aurora borealis. I've never been to Fair Isle, though I've wanted to since I was a girl. Our family has always had a special interest in handicrafts; in knitting and woolwork, in carpentry. So that maybe goes back to Fair Isle; to forebears who were knitters and boat builders. I presume it was hardship pushed them out. Orkney is very productive and fertile compared to Fair Isle. My grandfather took a small farm on the Isle of Westry. Then my father bought Papa Stronsay from his wife's brother, Tom Stout – in 1922 that was. And that's where I was born – Papa Stronsay.

Papa Stronsay is a small island that lies half a mile off Whitehall village, north-east of Stronsay. It's low and windswept but the soil is good and the grass grows well. It's roughly one mile long and half a mile wide with a fine tall farmhouse. My father worked the farm, collected kelp and ran the lighthouse, but the big thing, in those days, was the herring fishing. He organised all the onshore fishing work on Papa Stronsay. He made facilities available; he oversaw the building and renting out of the huts to the workers and the herring girls. I presume he controlled the harbour dues. There was a grocery store, a bakery, a butcher's and an ice-cream shop. That was more or less just a hole in the ground. We lived in the big house. The schoolteacher lodged with us, and three families of farmworkers lived in the farm cottages. So, in the 'thirties, the island had a

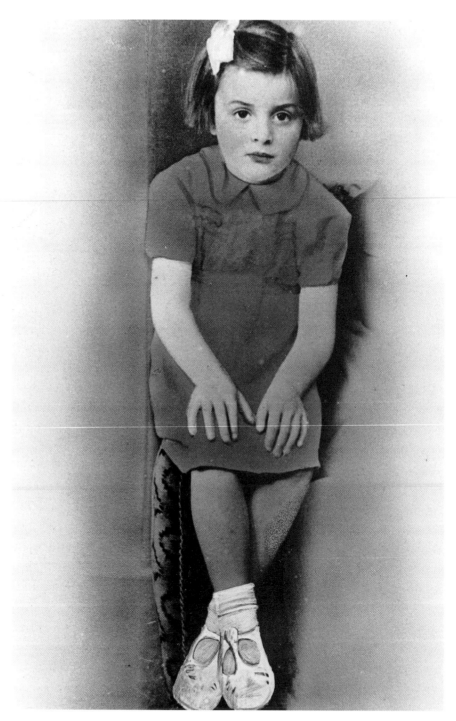

Margaret Dennison aged six. (MD)

basic population of about forty people. Then, every summer, we'd get another 600 people coming in for the fishing. With the fishermen off the boats at the weekends, that gave us well over 1,000 people on the island. Last year nobody was living on Papa Stronsay at all.

It's amazing for me to look back and know that I was a witness to

Margaret Dennison with her husband, Raymond, on Stronsay, Orkney, 1997. (MD)

that. I see Papa Stronsay every day from the farm here but I haven't landed for nearly thirty years. Charlie Smith has the island now. He has six or seven hundred sheep. He's married with children. They lived out there for about ten years, but recently they bought a house on the mainland of Stronsay and moved here. He goes across most days to see the sheep and do farm work, and the family sometimes goes over for a weekend and a few weeks in the summer but, for the first time in 6,000 years, Papa Stronsay is now uninhabited. The land was run down when Charlie bought it. He's got it in very good condition – but now it's up for sale. They want a bigger farm on the Stronsay mainland. And that's just what my father and brother-in-law wanted. And that's what they did. They worked Papa Stronsay until they could get a better farm on the mainland. Everybody seems to have used Papa Stronsay as a stepping stone to a permanent and more secure life on Stronsay itself. Maybe that's been going on since Bronze Age times. Papa Stronsay is a beautiful island but just too small for sustainable communities to develop and live at more than subsistence level. People today want more than subsistence. Papa Stronsay seems to have always attracted settlers and offered a challenge, but when the challenge has been met they move away. Usually they just came ashore to Stronsay, but sometimes they went much further afield, abroad. Challenge and response; island to mainland; flotsam and jetsam.

      The mainland of Stronsay seems to have had a stable population since Neolithic times, but the herring fishing pushed the population suddenly up to about 5,000 people. Now it's dropped back to between 350 people and 400. We are very

Top.
Charlie Smith, owner and farmer of
the island of Papa Stronsay, 1999.
(TN)

Bottom.
Papa Stronsay, inside the farm
buildings — hen roosting niches
and wool sacks, 1999. (TN)

Opposite top.
Papa Stronsay, limekilns with
nesting fulmar, 1999 (TN)

Papa Stronsay, house and farm building, 1998. (TN)

isolated. Until twenty years ago it still often took thirteen hours to reach Kirkwall on the mainland of Orkney! That was nothing to do with bad weather but because the mainland ferries circled the islands – one day in one direction and one day the other. So your voyage might take a few hours or it might take all day; and once you reached Kirkwall it took another full day to get to Scotland.

I'm not old enough to remember much of the old-style life on Papa Stronsay but it didn't differ much from life here on the main island. I remember the teacher who stayed in our house. I can just remember the fishing. We used to go down to the jetties – they were made of wood. I remember looking down and being fearful of the water beneath the gaps in the planks, and I remember being warned not to climb on the stacks of barrels waiting to be filled for export. They were like great pyramids to us children. I remember the day my mother died. I was eight. She had six children. My father quite soon then married her youngest sister and they had four children of their own. I was brought up in a family of ten. It was never strange for us, having a stepmother, because she was our aunt in the first place. Today four of those children are spread over the world but the rest live here on Stronsay.

By the time the Second World War got going, the fishing here was almost finished. The Papa Stronsay school was closed and I remember my

Papa Stronsay, house and farm buidings, 1998. (TN)

brothers coming home from Whitehall school by boat. It wasted a lot of my father's time, having to see them off and bring them back. So, with the herring days finished and with schooling made very difficult, my father decided to use the money he had from the herring years to buy Whitehall farm and move onto Stronsay. He didn't regret the move but he still liked to talk about Papa Stronsay.

        He told us about a big boat that was wrecked near the lighthouse. It was full of furniture and crockery. Many a house on Stronsay, to this day, still contains items from that ship. Another boat, full of scrap metal, set off from Sanday to go south. She had three men of a crew. There came a gale from the south-west. A week later it became known they had not turned up at their destination. A search was mounted round the shores here. One body was found at the point of the Ness – he was well above high water, so he must have been alive when he scrambled ashore but died of exhaustion. Another was found at the back of Bill Miller's and one on Papay, a very small island. He was found by this old wifie Mimie, Jimmy Stout's auntie. She lived on Stronsay. Her first job every morning was to go to the beach to see if there was any driftwood. She always liked to be first. That was the main hobby on Papa Stronsay – beachcombing. During the war the beachcombing was very good. A lot of wood came ashore and you got £1 for every mine you reported. My brother Tom found plenty. Most of them were about four feet in diameter and covered in horns, to trigger the explosive.

All the families on Papa Stronsay tried to be self-sufficient. Everybody had their own meal gunnel, a big wooden chest. You packed your oatmeal in one end and your beremeal in the other. That would keep you all winter – making your porridge, oatcakes, bere bannocks. We children were lifted up and put inside the gunnel to stamp the meal down. It had to be packed really hard. We thumped away in our knitted woollen socks. My mother made white mealie-puddings. We carefully laid them deep in the oatmeal: well packed they would stay good for months. I remember digging down with my mother to find them. We killed our own pigs, and we still do, and I still make mealie-puddings. My father had milking cattle and he bred beef, crossbred Shorthorn/Aberdeen Angus. Milk, butter, cheese, ice-cream: we made all those. We had hundreds and hundreds of hens. The chicken sheds were dotted about and spread all the way down to the lighthouse.

When I was a girl at Whitehall I became very friendly with an old lady who had been brought up on Papa Stronsay. She was a fish-gutter called Miss Robertson. She was very good to us children. When I was ten she gave me a bracelet, which I still have. And when the church was built she gifted the baptismal font and her name is on it. Jessie Chalmers was another of the fish-gutters. Everybody remembers Jessie Chalmers. She was a midwife and she used to come over in a rowing boat for all the births on Papa Stronsay. A midwife would not only deliver the baby but stay around for three weeks, keeping the mother in bed, looking after the baby and the house. That was still the custom here on Stronsay when I had my own eldest son. He's thirty-six. Mrs Burgess delivered him.

Jessie Chalmers was very dark skinned. Her husband was a cripple who worked as a cobbler. A very strong character she was: she organised the herring girls, she was the bread-winner, she ruled the roost. The herring work was hard but the women looked forward to it. There would be more than 1000 people promenading Whitehall village on a Saturday night. People enjoyed themselves. I heard it said that some weekends you could walk from Stronsay to Papa Stronsay across the decks of the moored boats. The pubs would be heaving. There were chip shops and a rest hut like a seaman's mission. But things changed on the Sunday – there was no work and no play on the Sunday.

Many of the fisher girls would come over from the West Coast. And there was a Sister, Sister Rae, who came with the girls. She worked for the Church of Scotland and she came back every year. She was their chaperone but also a nurse. She saw to the cuts on their hands and looked after their health. They wore bandages over their fingers for protection, but it was hard work and many a finger was lost among the herring. Most of these girls were new from school, just fourteen or fifteen years of age. They needed an eye. And the girls liked Sister Rae; she wasn't an ogre. I've heard of how they'd be coming down the street of a morning, her in the middle and the girls on each hand, all laughing and singing and enjoying themselves. A mother hen she was. They followed the fleet down, starting in Lerwick and going right down to Yarmouth. Short sleeves, long shirts and aprons; their forearms and hair silver-scaled from the herring. It was the summertime. I used to watch them going up for their ice creams at Stackaback, singing.

> I'm a rambling, rambling, fall da do da de
> I'm a rambling tambling lassie
> I'm a rambling, rambling, fall da do da de
> And they call me the fisherman's lassie.
>
> O the fisherman is a bold young man
> You'll never find anyone bolder
> He wears his seaboots over his knee
> And the straps across his shoulders.
>
> I'm a rambling, rambling, fall da do da de
> I'm a rambling tambling lassie
> I'm a rambling, rambling, fall da do da de
> And they call me the fisherman's lassie.
>
> I will dress myself in my Sunday best
> I'll make myself look bonnie
> Then I will high me up to the quay
> To greet my fair young Johnnie.
>
> I'm a rambling, rambling, fall da do da de
> I'm a rambling tambling lassie
> I'm a rambling, rambling, fall da do da de
> And they call me the fisherman's lassie.

Overleaf.
Fisher girls and fisher women, Papa Stronsay, c.1930. Midwife Jessie Chalmers is the swarthy woman, centre, fifth from right. (KM)

The farmers and the fisher people on Stronsay are separate but the local farm carts were very useful to the fishermen and they would be called into use, for rent, to move fish, the barrels – anything. That was an extra, cash in the hand for the farmers. But there was a big division between the two communities and I only remember one outside fisherwoman staying behind to marry a Stronsay man and that was Isla Chalmers – she belonged to Buckie.

And when I was eight two German girls came to work on the farm. After the war the government had a scheme to help young Germans without jobs or parents. The girls were very pleased to come to us. They told us that they'd been living on turnips for months. One worked in the house at Whitehall and the other worked outside on the land. They sent food parcels back to Germany. Two years they were here and neither went home. One went to Dundee to become a nurse, the other married a Stronsay man and they went off to America.

In the old days cattle were the main animals on Papa Stronsay. Sheep didn't thrive. There was a cobalt deficiency. Now that's all been sorted out and Charlie Smith builds up to 1200 sheep after lambing time. But in our day it would be fifteen to twenty cattle. They were taken out by barge, four to six at a time. We had just a few sheep. Horses would be swum across on a lead. You'd wait for a suitable tide and make for the lifeboat slip on Stronsay.

Papa Stronsay had good dykes to give shelter and catch the sun. The stone is good for building, as it is on Stronsay and as it is all over Orkney. There's been good building and good architecture on Orkney since the time of Skara Brae. Everything was well built on Papa Stronsay until they started putting up brick and concrete places in the time of the herring fishing. I like the style of the old dwelling houses on the island. Our house was built in the early nineteenth century. It's a tall house but only one room deep. That gave extra light. The top floor was for the servants, two men and two girls. The farm stands like a castle. That's also true of the farms on Stronsay. They mostly stand on a knoll, and, at a distance, the house and the steadings look like one single building, like a hillfort. That's what they must have been to begin with. All the byres conjoin to make one silhouette like a fortress against the wind.

It was the roll-on roll-off ferries that put an end to the cattle on Papa Stronsay. Today the ferries only work out of Whitehall, out of the one main harbour on each of the big islands on Orkney – but the old boats would call at Papa Stronsay and take the cattle straight off. And they would call at all the small islands. The trip to Kirkwall might take thirteen hours but once the cattle were loaded you were all right, but today, with the insurance and safety regulations being what they are, no ships call at the small islands at all.

Orkney beef is often said to be the best in the world and Orkney lamb is good, but since the BSE and scrapie scares the economy of farming is not sustainable in outlying places like Stronsay. Lambs sent from Shetland to Aberdeen in 1997 were fetching £1, and it cost £3 per lamb, freight! I work as a nursery teacher and it's clear that the government is more interested in education for four-year-olds than it is in sorting out the beef crisis. That's something, but, in my opinion, that's the wrong priority in a place like Orkney. It's no good looking after the children if you're destroying the men. I run the playgroup for three to five-

year-olds. But I'm also a farmer's wife and I know what's truly important.

I think John Major was a disaster – all that huffing and puffing about rescinding the beef ban or else! Four years have passed and we're still where we were! But we're not for this Scottish Nationalism here, either. Things are different in Orkney and Shetland. We've got a lot of incomers here and what would this island be without them? It's not just that they help keep the economy and community going – but it's a fact – there'd be very few Orcadians left at all if it wasn't for the newcomers keeping up the school numbers. I say long may it continue. They're the reason why we've still got education up to sixteen on Stronsay. You can go to Kirkwall at fourteen – or you can stay here. That's good, but the problem is jobs; there's not enough jobs. Tourism has overtaken farming as the main industry on Orkney. That's good for the mainland of Orkney but tourism hardly touches us here in Stronsay. We pull in some 'twitchers' but that's about it. The secret is to announce you've seen a 'thing-a-me-bob' … and people will rush in from all over! The possible sighting of a rare bird brings the people and the media flocking from all over Europe – whilst the sight of farmers killing and burying flocks of unsellable sheep goes by like the snow. And people in Eastern Europe are hungry and people in Africa starving!

And all this legislation about hygiene! It's forcing the small farmer and the small producers out of business. Years ago you just got on with it. We had our own milk, we made our own cheese. If you were milking the cows and your fingers got sticky you just dipped them in the milk. It didn't hurt the cow and it didn't hurt us. In the long term I expect the chemical and biological cleansers will do far more harm than water and soap. Today when we take the nursery children or the school children out to a farm they all have to be issued with protective clothing. It costs a great deal of money and those clothes are used maybe once a year. The Stronsay children have been in and out of byres for 5000 years! The danger here is not getting cow muck on a child's boots but going into a byre and finding the farmer hanging from a rafter.

To change the subject. The tinkers used to come out to Stronsay every summer. I even heard they went out to Papa Stronsay. Some would have tents and stay up by the kirkyard; some would take a cottage or stay in outbuildings. Most came from the Orkney mainland but some came down from Shetland. Newlands and MacPhees, many of them. They came with their ponies and traps. Later they came in cars and vans. We had one here just three weeks ago, from Fraserburgh. He must have been related to the ones that used to come years ago. He looked like them and he spoke like them. The same accent, the same very fast speech, the same slanty eyes – and very interesting to speak to. He had a new Mini. He said he was looking for scrap: lead, brass, copper. In the old days the woman would come dressed in rags and sleep on the straw. But I don't think they

were all poor. It was their style. And I never met anyone so persistent at the door. Never letting go of the bone! Talk, talk, talk – till you agreed with or would do anything to get rid of them! But they didn't like it if you came too close to their camp. The Newlands sold mainly drapery and pots and the MacPhees made tin.

There are three Bronze Age archaeological sites on Papa Stronsay. A skeleton was found in the Earl's Mound and, from the size of the thighs, it was said to be the body of a man eight foot five inches tall! By the beach to the north-west of the main farmhouse there's a walled field for corn. It's like a natural amphitheatre and it was there that Thorfinn killed Jarl Rognvald in single combat and won control of all Orkney.

As one of the most easterly of the Orkney islands, Stronsay is a refuge for huge numbers of migrating birds and very rare birds. We have fine cliffs, numerous caves, bonksies, puffins, guillemots, razorbills, arctic terns, gulls of every kind. There's the Kirbister Arch and down at the south end a whole village of Pictish houses. When we were young we used to climb inside the biggest house and crawl in a circle through all the chambers. One hole led down into a sea cave, so the inhabitants could escape if they were attacked or besieged.

Along the bird cliffs stand two towers of rock, called 'Tam's Castles'. Tam was a hermit and on one rock he built himself a garden and on the other he built himself a house like a hermitage; a primitive bungalow with four rooms and a stone-walled veranda, front and back, to catch the morning sun and the evening sun, and to stop himself falling to his death! He lived, it seems, on fish and seabirds and whatever he could grow in the garden tower. I think it was about 100 years ago he lived there. So there we have it: 'Tam's Rock', Papa Stronsay, Stronsay, Orkney – all variations on the theme of a hard life. Looking back it is the herring girls I remember best – working, walking and singing.

O vhat'll we do with a herring's heid?
Vhat'll we do with a herring's heid?
We'll mak it for love? We'll sell it for breid
Herring's heid and lobster breid
And all these thochts o things —
For all the fish that swim in the sea
The herring it is the fish for me.

Sing! Alla la ligo, alla la ligo
      Alla la li lay …

O vhat'll we do with a herring's eyes?
Vhat'll we do with a herring's eyes?
We'll mak em for puddings, we'll sell em for pies
Herring's eyes, puddings and pies
Herring's heid, lobster breid
And all these thochts o things —
For all the fish that swim in the sea
The herring is the fish for me.

Sing! Alla la ligo, alla la ligo
      Alla la li lay.

O vhat'll we do with a herring's fins?
Vhat'll we do with a herring's fins?
We'll mak em for needles we'll sell em for pins
Herring's fins, needles and pins
Herring's eyes, puddings and pies
Herring's heid, lobster breid
And all these thochts o things –
For all the fish that swim in the sea
The herring it is the fish for me.

Sing! Alla la ligo, alla la ligo
       Alla la li lay.

O vhat'll we do with a herring's back?
Vhat'll we do with a herring's back?
We'll mak it a laddie, we'll christen it Jack
Herring's back, Laddie ca'd Jack
Herring's fins, needles and pins
Herring's eyes, puddings and pies
Herring's heid, lobster breid
And all these thochts o things –
For all the fish that swim in the sea
The herring it is the fish for me.

Sing! Alla la ligo, alla la ligo
       Alla la li lay.

And vhat'll we do with a herring's belly
Vhat'll we do with a herring's belly
We'll mak it a lassie, we'll christen it Nellie
Herring's belly, lassie ca'd Nellie
Herring's back, Laddie ca'd Jack
Herring's fins, needles and pins
Herring's eyes, puddings and pies
Herring's heid, lobster breid
And all these thochts o things —
For all the fish that swim in the sea
The herring it is the fish for me.

Sing! Alla la ligo, alla la ligo
    Alla la li lay.

And vhat'll we do with a herring's tail
Vhat'll we do with a herring's tail
We'll mak it a ship, with a beautiful sail
Herring's tail, a ship with a sail
Herring's belly, lassie ca'd Nellie
Herring's back, Laddie ca'd Jack
Herring's fins, needles and pins
Herring's eyes, puddings and pies
Herring's heid, lobster breid
And all these thochts o things —
For all the fish that swim in the sea
The herring it is the fish for me.

Sing! Alla la ligo, alla la ligo
    Alla la li lay.

Previous page.
Papa Stronsay in the mid-morning
sun, 1999. (TN)

Above.
Charlie Smith, Papa Stronsay,
1999. (TN)

We don't hear much of that kind of singing on Stronsay nowadays – but we *will* hear singing. Papa Stronsay has been bought – by an order of monks! Eighteen brothers have come; they're already over there. They belong to the Transalpine Redemptionists. They're very traditional – they refuse to accept the modernisation of the Roman Catholic Church; they continue to sing the old Latin mass. They've bought the whole island and all the rights; they've bought our old house, the farm steading, the cottages, all 600 of Charlie Smith's sheep; everything.

We've seen some of the monks – they all wear black habits – but we've not met them. There's been a lot about the sale in the papers. Papa is old Norse for 'priest' and Latin for 'father'. So the monks are very pleased with the name of their island. But the Italian teacher here, Mary Acheson, she was telling us that Stronsay translates as 'bastard' in Italian – which is not quite so suitable!

However, I don't think that will worry them — they follow a man called St Alphonsus and the Order is based in France. For six months each year they practise prayer and solitude, then for six months they go out into the community and work in parish missions. We hear they may rebuild the ruined chapel. They still sing the old style Gregorian chants. We should be able to hear their voices drifting across the water. The island is an ancient holy site, so its new purpose brings history full-circle.

The head man is brother Nicholas Mary. He says the island's idyllic, a 'monastic paradise'. The *Daily Mail* reported him as saying: 'Our community believes in solitude and we should find all the solitude we need on this island — and more. In a world of phones and fax machines it is almost impossible to find a place where you can rest your head in heaven but keep your feet firmly on the ground — but here, on Papa Stronsay, we can do that. Here we have found it.' I think that's very nice and I hope the monks make a great success of their life on the island. Maybe they'll stay for hundreds of years. I welcome the monks just as I welcome the outsiders here. It's a pity they won't have children! But the world's not short of children; it's only short of beautiful spaces like Papa Stronsay, short of people willing to work in fields like these, like the monks, like my husband and our sons.

Neil MacGillivray

BURG AND INCHKENNETH ON THE ISLAND OF MULL

'She said she would need a ferryman in the next life,
just as much as she needed one in this.'

Looking at a photograph of me when young and looking at me now, aged eighty-four, you'd never think I was a man who often danced with Hitler's mistress. That was Unity Mitford. Both she and her mother were very fond of me. They lived here on Mull, on the island of Inchkenneth. I was boatman and general manager of the island – but it's a long story and it seems a very long time ago.

I was born at Butterstone, by Dunkeld in Perthshire, but my father's people were all from Mull, from Burg, over there on the Ardmeanach peninsula. It's a very isolated place and a very beautiful place and looks south over Loch Scravaig. No one lives there now, just backpackers moving through, but Burg is an old settlement that once had plenty of good arable ground. The trouble was there was no proper road and there's still no road beyond Tavool. There was just the one big farm –Burg farm – when I went out in 1928. It belonged to a man called Turner. He then sold it to Blair Campbell, who gifted it to the National Trust for Scotland. That was in 1932. It was one of the very first properties they took on. Burg farm consisted of 1525 acres, mostly moorland, but the coastline is volcanic and spectacular. It was the landscape the Trust wanted, but they decided to keep the farm going and I worked at Burg all through the 'thirties and the War – but by the 'fifties the farm was no longer viable. The old folk were dying. Everything was in decline, so when I got the offer to be boatman and general manager of the island of Inchkenneth I left. That was in 1952.

There's no one living out at Burg today, but I pay the National Trust a nominal rental for the old corrugated house we lived in and I still go out once a month to keep an eye on the place with my daughter, Chrissie. The old farmhouse where my grandparents lived is now used as a bothy when parties of

Opposite.
Neil MacGillivray, aged 84,
penning sheep for market, Aird of
Kinloch, Mull, 1999. (TN)

This page, top.
Neil MacGillivray's grandmother
and grandfather, Isabella
MacDonald, Malcolm MacGillivray,
Mrs Graham of Buneran, her son,
Neil Duncan Graham. In the front
row are Neil MacGillivray and his
pal Andy Graham. (The grandmother
of Isabella MacDonald was Mary
MacDonald, composer of the carol
'Child in a Manger', Lennaich
Each). Burg, 1925. (NM)

This page, bottom.
Shearing at Burg, c.1932.
J. Lamont, J. Telfer, D. MacGillivray,
Lawson Bell, Neil MacGillivray,
kneeling front right.
(NM)

volunteers visit to carry out maintenance, though it's had very little done for many years. It's about eight miles from the croft here, at the Aird of Kinloch, to the Burg steadings. I don't like to see the place falling apart. Burg and Inchkenneth are the two places I think of as home. Out beyond Burg above Camus an Fheidh, you'll see the two big waterfalls and famous fossil tree. Burg gets its name from an iron-age fort – Dun Bhuirg – and Ardmeanach is dotted with ancient hut circles, burial cairns and field systems.

My grandfather was Malcolm MacGillivray, my mother was Isabella MacDonald. Her grandmother was Mary MacDonald, the composer. She wrote 'Child in a Manger' ('Leannaich Each'), and many other songs. I think it's that side of my family I mostly take after. Hugh MacGillivray, my father, was born at Burg, but left about 1900 to find paid work. He became a gardener on Loch Etiveside. That's where he met my mother – she was a domestic servant who'd come up from England. Her name was French – Annie Elizabeth French. From Loch Etive they moved across to work at the big house at Butterstone, but every summer we came back to Burg for holidays – staying with my grandparents and my auntie and uncle and, as soon as I left school, I started work on the Burg farm. In fact I came back before I left school, when I was twelve years old. It was always Burg, not Butterstone, that felt like home to me. I wasn't brought up speaking Gaelic, but I'd always heard Gaelic and out there with Gaelic all round it was only weeks before I was speaking the language like a native. Little else was spoken here in those days. At Burg we had cattle and we had plenty of sheep, horses. We had hay, oats and barley. We had a boat and went fishing. For a young man like me it seemed the ideal life. We had little enough money but we had what we needed. The Great Depression in Glasgow, in Perth, in Dundee passed us by.

One of the things I remember about Perthshire was the number of tinkers. They were a very noticeable part of the scenery. Dunkeld, Butterstone, Logierait, Ballinluig, at school – Stewarts and Reids were everywhere. Keeping themselves apart and tough as nails. As soon as a tinker baby was born he was plunged naked in running water. They were taken straight from the mother and held under fast flowing water. That would be the Tay or the Tummel or the Tilt, or just any small burn they were camped beside. Summer, wintertime, midwinter, it didn't matter – that's what they did. It washed the bairn clean but it must have been some kind of test – to get rid of the weaklings – like the Spartans putting their boys out, overnight, on the mountain. It was a baptism into the hard school of Nature. There was a big camp at Birnam, it was called 'The Tinker's Widdie', hidden in amongst the trees.

There was an old chap called Donald Reid who had a pony and trap and who went to the pub every Saturday night. I remember him standing there outside the pub, drinking, one swig for himself and one for the pony – straight out of the bottle. All the tinkers had something of the showman about them. Saturday night was the night of the battle and they were real battles. There was a big feud going on in those days between the Stewarts and the Townsleys. The two sides would line up, taunting each other, then go for it, hammer and tongs. I watched them myself. We had them up at Butterstone and they had them down on the Inches at Perth. You don't see tinkers here on Mull these days but they used to visit; they'd come here picking whelks. And it's a strange thing, you can

Opposite top.
Shearing at the fank at Tavool, next
farm to Burg, c.1890. I. Cowan,
J. Lamont, J. Cowan, Jean Allan,
Malcolm MacHarney, Jago MacNeil,
J. Clark. (NM)

Opposite bottom.
Neil Duncan, Neil's grandfather,
on stack, with neighbours from
Tavool, Burg, 1916. (NM)

Above.
Burg. The sheep pens in front of the
Burg farmhouse in which Neil
MacGillivray's grandparents lived,
c.1934. Neil is on the right.

Opposite.
Neil MacGillivray renewing the
road to Tirovan, 1933. (NM)

always recognise them. See one – and you know the race for ever. They have this look about them. Here on Mull, maybe, I didn't see tinkers for twenty years, but as soon as I saw them again, I recognised them – at 100 yards. There's something about their gait, their features. I'd say they tend to be squat, thickset, and the Reids were red-haired.

Well, I lived and worked at Burg from 1927 till after the war. At that time the country needed all the food it could get, so I was in a reserved occupation and there was no question of me going away in the Forces. I was the only youngster at Burg, so a lot of the heavy work fell on me, but I was strong and I enjoyed that. Beyond our family, MacGillivrays and Grahams, there was one old-timer, John MacRae. Things weren't easy. Old Mrs Graham had thirteen children and every one of them died before she did, two brothers being burned to death in a boat shed at Bunessan. We tried hard to keep things going. With the new Labour government in 1945, Burg was selected as a site for special experiments to clear the bracken that was then invading the fields reclaimed off the hills. Those experiments went very well. We got rid of the bracken and we grew good crops but, in the end, nothing much seemed to come of it. I would say one of the best things the new Scottish Parliament could do would be to wage war on bracken, because the problem's getting worse and worse.

I got married in 1947, on 18th December, in the Kennedy Tearooms in Oban. A minister officiated. My wife's name was Janet, but she was always called Netta. We went back out to Burg, but it was very isolated for a young wife with bairns, so when I saw this advertisement in the *Oban Times* for

the job on Inchkenneth, I went for it. I'd known the island since the days of my boyhood. It was just a short sail up the coast from Burg – eight or nine miles – often enough we rowed up. Inchkenneth is a beautiful, fertile island and there was a good modern bungalow for us to live in, about sixty yards from the main house. So, I got the job and we lived there on Inchkenneth for nineteen years. That's where my family grew up. We were very happy there. We went away for six years, to try a new life in Australia, but we came back to Inchkenneth. My wife wanted home. The dry air in Queensland was very bad for her tonsillitis and Lady Redesdale was always writing, encouraging us to come back to the island. So we returned.

For years I ferried the children every day to the school at Griben. Later they all went away to board at Oban High School. On Inchkenneth I ran the boats, I ran the farm, I looked after the generator and all the machinery. We had everything we wanted and for eight months a year we would have the whole island to ourselves. We had a walled garden, beautiful fruit and vegetables. We could gather wild oysters on the shore and watercress from the spring. It was idyllic in many ways and I'd be there yet if things had turned out otherwise.

Lady Redesdale would normally come just for the summer months. We got on very well. She trusted us in everything. She brought her family and plenty of visitors and we enjoyed their coming. That was our life for nineteen years, until Lady Redesdale died and the island was sold. She depended on us. I think I can say that she loved our family. In fact, she used to say she wouldn't die unless I promised to go with her. She used to say she would need a ferryman in the next life, just as much as she needed one in this. It was like a pharaoh wishing to be buried with his servants and all the accoutrements of life! Although she'd had a big family she was, in some ways, very lonely and her family had been beset with tragedies – just like the Kennedys in America. She was a Bowles who married into the Mitford family, the Redesdales. Her husband was Lord Redesdale. He'd bought Inchkenneth a short time before the outbreak of the Second World War. At about the same time he decided to run off with his secretary and he never visited the island during my time. He was a great pal of both kings, George V and George VI, and usually stayed in a house down in Kent.

Lady Redesdale had been a famous hostess in London, between the wars, and a lot of her friends came up here. Arnold Toynbee came. He wrote books on the theory of civilisation. His son Philip came (very sharp tempered he was, with both his wives!), his daughter Polly – she came. She writes for *The Guardian* and is a big Tony Blair supporter, very ambitious for ennoblement. The Redesdales were friends with John Betjeman and Evelyn Waugh. The rooms of Inchkenneth House were full of books. Lady Redesdale would quote the poem, *The Ship of Death,* by D. H. Lawrence:

> Have you built your ship of death, O have you?
> O build your ship of death, for you will need it …
>
> Already the dark and endless ocean of the end
> Is washing through the breaches of our wounds,
> Already the flood is upon us.
>
> O build your ship of death, your little ark
> And furnish it with food, with little cakes, and wine
> For the dark flight down oblivion …
>
> A little ship, with oars and food
> And little dishes, and all accoutrements
> Fitting and ready for the departing soul …
>
> O build your ship of death. O build it!
> For you will need it.
> For the voyage of oblivion awaits you.

We all like poetry in our family. When the children went away to Oban High School they were lucky – they were taught by Iain Crichton Smith, the novelist and Gaelic poet. He died just recently. He was given a pretty hard time in Oban, the children nicknamed him, 'Willie the Weed'! They used to say he had a nervous breakdown every day. The headmaster, John MacLean, who was a great Classics scholar, was heard to say that Mr Crichton Smith was the cleverest man he'd ever met. He was a genius, but that didn't make any difference to the school kids. They laughed him to scorn. But later he found his freedom – he got married to a nurse and they went to live at Taynault. He became famous in Scotland. All five of my children remember him as clear as day. My son, James, is a ship's engineer. He reads Crichton Smith out there in the South Atlantic, off Brazil, drilling for oil. One poem is called *Tha Thu Air Aieann M'Inntinn*:

Gun fhios dhomh tha thu air aigeann m'inntinn
Mar fhear-tadhail grunnd na mara
Le chlogaid's a dha shuil mhoir
'S chan aithne dhomh ceart d'fhiamh do dhoigh
An deidh coig bliadhn shiantan
Time doradh eadar mise's tu:

Beanntan buirn gun aiinm a'dortadh
Eadar mise 'gad shlaoddadh air bord
'S d'fhaimh 's do dhoighean b'nam lamhan fann.
Chaidh thu air chall
Am measg lusan diumhair a' ghrunna
Anns an leth-sholus uaine gbun ghradh,

'S chan eirich thu chaoidh air bharr cuain
A chaoidh 's mo lamhan a'slaodadh gun sgur
'S chan aithne dhomh do shlighe idir,
Thus'ann an leth-sholus do shuain
A 'tathaich aigenann na mara gun tamh
'S mise slaodadh 's a'slaodadh air uachdar cuain.

YOU ARE AT THE BOTTOM OF MY MIND

Without my knowing it you are at the bottom of my mind
Like a visitor to the bottom of the sea
With his helmet and his two large eyes
And I do not rightly know your appearance or your manner
After five years of showers
Of time pouring between me and you:

Nameless mountains of water pouring
Between me hauling you on board
And your appearance and manner in my weak hands.
You went astray
Among the mysterious plants of the sea-bed
In the green half-light without love,

And you will never rise to the surface
Though my hands are hauling ceaselessly
And I do not know your way at all,
You in the half-light of your sleep
Haunting the bed of the sea without ceasing
And I hauling and hauling on the surface.

We didn't go out to live on Inchkenneth till 1952, but I was a regular over there
long before that. Many summers I went across to help with the harvest, and Lady
Redesdale's daughters used to come across shopping and to dances at Gribun
school. Married or unmarried, they'd all join in. I think I'll now be one of the last
men on Mull who can say they danced with Hitler's mistress! That was Unity. She
was the fourth daughter. She came to live on the island in 1944 and never left till
she was on her deathbed. She had an assistant, a helper, called Marieanna.

The Redesdales were very rich, very brilliant and very eccentric.
There were six daughters and one son, Tom. He was killed fighting the Japs in
Burma. Nancy Mitford was the eldest. She lived in Paris, married to a man called
Peter Rodd. It was Nancy who wrote the book called *The U Cult*. It became very
fashionable, about proper behaviour, manners; about status and class; about what
distinguishes those who consider themselves to be the upper class. All books
about being 'U' and 'non-U' go back to Nancy. Many was the time I ferried her
to and from Inchkenneth.

The second daughter was Diana. She was said to be the most
beautiful. She married Bryan Guinness, one of the millionaire controllers of the

Inchkenneth House, c.1959. (BB)

Dublin brewers. She lived the wild life of a thirties socialite and she fell in love with Oswald Mosley – the British Fascist leader. She became one of his mistresses, then when his wife died, she married him. She had his children and she's stayed loyal to him all her life. She was frequently on Inchkenneth but, for some reason, Mosley never crossed the water. He always stayed in the house on the shore at Gribun, opposite the island. I didn't meet him myself but local people have told me that Mosley was quite a fine man – to meet, to talk to, and I always got on very well with Diana. She's still alive today, in her ninetieth year.

After Diana came Jessica, who we all called 'Decca'. She married a nephew of Sir Winston Churchill – I think that's who it was. She'd become a communist and the two of them ran away to fight in the Spanish Civil War for the Republicans. It was said the British Government sent a warship after them, to bring them back, but they got away and stayed out there driving ambulances until he was killed. I think that's right because after that Decca went off to America,

where she met and married a man called Truhart. He was another communist. I met him several times. Decca often came back to Inchkenneth and she wrote her most famous book, *The American Way of Death,* on Inchkenneth. One of her books is based upon her own family – it's called *Hons and Rebels.* They were a very divided family. The two main characters are called Farve and Muv, being based on her mother and father, Lord and Lady Redesdale.

  The fifth daughter was Pamela. She became Mrs Jackson. She was the least exceptional. We used to say that she was the only one that was normal! But Jackson was another very wealthy man. He was a brewer, a very wealthy brewer. He came from another of the old brewing families, like the Guinnesses.

  Last came Deborah. I knew her very well. She married the Duke of Devonshire. We got an invitation to Chatsworth for the wedding. They were all very good to us. We couldn't go. Deborah's politics will be Tory, I presume. So there we are – a very strange family. 'Some chicken, some neck!' as Winston Churchill said.

Unity was the strangest of them all. She was the fourth daughter and she was born in August 1914, the month the Great War broke out. Her first name, Unity, must have been a plea for peace, but her second name was Valkyrie, a very Wagnerian and very warlike name. She was a beautiful, Teutonic, Aryan-looking woman. She went off to Germany in the 'thirties and fell in love with Hitler and the Third Reich. She lived a hectic life in Munich, courting and being courted by the fashionable aristocratic élite. Her nickname was 'Bobo'. She and Eva Braun were Hitler's two favourites. Hitler tried to use her to build fences with Britain. I've read that the happiest moment of her life was 'sitting at the Führer's feet while he stroked her hair'. She used to speak of how beautiful and blue his eyes were. How much he liked chocolate éclairs. She's supposed to have reported, 'He abstained from sex,' but if Unity didn't have sex with Hitler she certainly enjoyed it with others. She had a racing MG, open-top, and used to drive around in low-cut dresses, singing; flags and pennants streaming behind her on the Alpine roads. She had an affair with Count Almacy, the German spy on whom the novel and the film *The English Patient* is based. After bedtime prayers, it's said, she would give a Nazi salute before jumping into bed. Of course, that was long before she came here to Inchkenneth.

When I knew her she sometimes had difficulty walking. You see it came as a terrible shock for Unity when war was declared on 3rd September 1939. That same day she went out into the English Garden in Munich and shot herself in the head. The two nations she loved were at war. She left a note to the Führer: 'Be merciful to my people.' She must have assumed Hitler all-powerful. The bullet lodged in her brain. She was rushed to hospital but the bullet was not retrievable. Very slowly she recuperated with the bullet still there in her head, until, on the Führer's personal orders, she was evacuated through Switzerland back to Britain. Doctors said, at best, she would live ten years, and that's what she did.

Lady Redesdale wanted to bring her up to Inchkenneth to convalesce in tranquillity, but Loch na Keal, the sea loch in which Inchkenneth lies, was an important naval anchorage and the security people thought she might radio information to the enemy. So it was not till 1944, after the invasion of Europe, and shortly after her sister Diana was released from prison, that she was brought north. Although, once the war started, Mosley urged his Fascist followers to join up and fight against Hitler, he was not trusted and both he and Diana were imprisoned for four years. Still, once Unity arrived she spent the rest of her life on Inchkenneth. She would walk in the garden and sit for hours on the pier, wrapped in a blanket, looking out to sea. And she would come over to the post office at Gribun, and she would come over for dances at the school. That's when I would dance with her. The boatman on Inchkenneth then was Baldy

MacFadyan, but sometimes, late at night, I would ferry her back to the island and we got on very well.

There's a very old chapel on the island and when visitors came they would sometimes hold services there. Later on I used to read the lesson myself. She was only thirty-four when she died. It was John MacFadyan who brought her back over the water for the last time and she was carried on a stretcher and put on the ferry at Craignure and taken up to the cottage hospital in Oban. The death certificate states that she died from an 'old gunshot wound'. Her death came within weeks of the ten years that the German doctors had originally diagnosed, and four years after Hitler shot himself in the bunker.

Many people will say she deserved all she got, and Hitler deserved much worse than he got. However, it's still a tragic story.

She had a small bedroom on the second floor of the house, but her bed was a grand four-poster with sagging green drapes, pale and worn thin with age. She was not Fascist when I knew her. She and her mother used to entertain the local children at Gribun with parties at Eastertime, and I remember watching her in the kitchen, cracking eggs to make a cake. She had become absent-minded and she just kept cracking eggs – three or four dozen she cracked into a great bowl and then whipped them up. I didn't say anything. I was not employed on the island at that time; I was just helping out with the boats, so I said nothing.

Inchkenneth certainly has a colourful and chequered history. Before the Mitfords it was the Boltons who had the island. They were textile millionaires from the north of England. Lady Bolton was an alcoholic and Sir Harold Bolton bought Inchkenneth as refuge and sanctuary for her – he hoped to wean her off the booze! She came up with her sister and the idea was that, marooned on the island, they would learn to live without drink. Of course, the opposite happened: the two women got themselves organised. It wasn't long before small boats were bringing them all they needed. More than they needed! My boys were still finding secret stashes of whisky in the late 'fifties: bottles hidden in niches in the garden wall, whole crates buried down by the well! There's a story they once hid two bottles of whisky under the central heating boiler. When the gardener lit up next morning, the bottles exploded, setting fire to the whole shed!

It was the Boltons who made the last major renovations to Inchkenneth House. It's a nineteenth-century baronial type building adapted in the 'thirties. It's part Highland castle, part country house and part art deco mansion – that's the quality the Boltons added. They waterproofed and upgraded the whole building. Sir Harold built a private chapel, next to the bedrooms on the top floor. It must have been part of his plan to reform the wife. It had an altar with a statue of the Virgin Mary, but one day, very drunk or in a fit of anger, Lady Bolton picked up the statue and flung it out the window. It's very lucky no

Marian and Peter Campbell (gardener), Janet MacGillivray, Lady Redesdale, Lady Redesdale's maid, James MacGillivray with Prince, Kenneth and Robert with Sheltie, Linda on Cherry Blossom, Neil MacGillivray, c. 1959. Inchkenneth with Mull in the background. (BB)

bootlegger was passing! The statue shattered on the paving slabs by the front door and shot off into the grass in a thousand pieces. We were still finding bits thirty years later!

The builders for the Boltons did a good job. By adding a bow front to the house they created more light and beautiful views all through 180 degrees. The long drawing room on the first floor is a splendid room and such a big room is rare in a Highland castle. It's got a handsome stone fireplace that I used to keep going with driftwood – the whole family would go down to the shore collecting with a cart. None of the Inchkenneth bedrooms are en suite – not like you get in most bed-and-breakfast places these days – but there were plenty of big bathrooms and toilets just across the passageways. The house gets very damp through the winter these days, but it was a fine house to live in when we were there. The whole island is well sheltered and you get something of a microclimate in Loch na Keal. I remember the spring of 1963, when all Britain was locked in ice and snow – we escaped almost unscathed and March was beautiful. We basked

in warm sunshine whilst all Scotland shivered. We followed it on the radio.

After the death of Unity, the Redesdales only came for summer holidays, so for nine months of the year we had the island to ourselves. We killed a sheep occasionally; we killed a pig every year. We salted down the hams. We made our own brine, using a little sugar, then adding salt till the solution would float a fresh, raw potato. We had several dairy cows. They gave us all the milk we needed and plenty of butter and cheese. The soil on Inchkenneth is lime rich and very fertile, unlike Mull and so much of the Highlands. Where geological faults thrust up lime-rich rock you always get excellent fertile soils – as on Tiree and Lismore, and Inchkenneth. Nature is a wonderful thing. They say the mountains are still growing in Scotland.

The house garden was close by our bungalow. It was sheltered by a wall and by a hillock rising to the north and by two lines of sycamore trees. We grew good vegetables, strawberries, raspberries. We made jam. We kept two horses and a pony. We had several good arable fields. We harvested by hand,

The MacGillivray family in front of Inckenneth house, c. 1959. Neil, Netta, James, Robert, Kenneth and Linda on Cherry Blossom. (BB)

binding the sheaves; stooking, stacking. During the Great War they used to bring quite a number of men over from Mull for the harvest – seventeen I think it was – but by the Second World War it was just two or three, and in our time I could manage on my own, with the children. But we liked it like that.

Both cattle and sheep were sent away for the sales. It was never easy getting animals on or off Inchkenneth, but it had to be done. Lambs would go in a boat, but the cattle and horses had to swim. It's not difficult at a big, equinoctial low tide. We'd wait for calm weather and drive them out, reef by reef, then head 75 degrees east from Inchkenneth. You had to know the banks, but with us the old cows would have made the journey many times – they used to lead the way. If we were just taking two cows across to the bull at Balmeanach, we'd tie them behind a dinghy and row them across. We only had one drowning in my time. The wind got up and a big bullock panicked, broke away and drowned. We got the body ashore and we skinned it there and then on the rocks, quartered it and took it home. 'Rat beef' we called it and very good it was. Today most people are afeared to swim cattle because of the Animal Rights people – they'd be on you like a shot. But in our time we had no trouble with anything like that. Inchkenneth was a great place to bring up a family: five children we had – James, Robert, Kenneth, Catherine and Linda.

And Inchkenneth is a very healthy place and a safe place, like Iona. In fact the whole west of Mull is a very healthy place. Last year I climbed Ben More for charity. You see, my wife, Netta, died of cancer, so I like to help raise money. I plan to go up again in the Millennium year – that will be my eighty-seventh year. The sea air has kept me healthy all these year. TB was never bad with us here on Mull – but I was thinking, just the other day, about smallpox. We had one of the last outbreaks of smallpox, in 1891. Two whole families went down with the disease, out by Bunessan. It was a fearful disease in those days, and those families were shunned by their neighbours. There was no doctor nearby, but a passing stranger cared for them, a pedlar. He nursed both families through their illnesses and they recovered. He then went on his way to Craignure, but there, by a small pool at the roadside, he took very ill himself. He didn't go into the village, or ask for help: he just lay down by the road and died there by the pool. When his body was found it was buried on the spot, with his pack beside him. The men burnt their shovels. But that place is still known as 'the Pedlar's Pool' and a small cairn was raised surmounted with an iron Celtic cross. You can still see it to this day. None of the monks of Iona did more for the sick than that old pedlar-man. I often think about him.

Like Iona, Inchkenneth has been inhabited for thousands of years. The monks on Iona used it as a granary, and because it's an island sheltered from the open Atlantic, it's always been used as a port in a storm. Many kings, princes and nobles were buried on Inchkenneth when the weather prevented a landing on Iona. In the Medieval period the island was the home to a nunnery, a sister foundation to St Columba's monastery on Iona. In the eighteenth century it was home to the MacLean chief, Sir Allan MacLean, who was knighted after service in the Seven Years War. Although Mull had been MacLean territory for hundreds of years, it was taken over by the Dukes of Argyll in the seventeenth century and Sir Allan had to lease Inchkenneth from Argyll. Boswell and Johnston stayed a week on Inchkenneth during their Hebridean tour and it was an amazing pocket of civilisation they found there. We have the books and they're well worth reading, I like Boswell, especially.

As we walked from the shore, Dr Johnson's heart was cheered by the sight of a road marked with cart wheels, as on the mainland; a thing we had not seen for a long time. It gave us a pleasure similar to that which a traveller feels when, whilst wandering on what he fears is a desert island, he perceives the print of human feet.

Military men acquire excellent habits of having all conveniences about them. Sir Allan MacLean, who had long been in the army, and had now a lease of this island, had formed a commodious habitation, though it consisted of but a few small buildings, only one storey high. He had, in his little apartments, more things than I could enumerate in a page or two ...

Dr Johnson here showed so much of the spirit of a Highlander that he won Sir Allan's heart; indeed he has shown it during the whole of our tour. One night in Coll he strutted about the room with a broadsword and targe, and made a formidable appearance; and another night I took the liberty to put a large blue bonnet on his head. His age, size, and his bushy grey wig with this covering on it, presented the image of a venerable sennachie; and, however unfavourable to the Lowland Scots, he seemed much pleased to assume the appearance of an ancient Caledonian. We only regretted that he could not be prevailed with to partake of the social glass. One of his arguments against drinking appears to me not convincing. He urged that in proportion as drinking makes a man different from what he was before he has drunk, it is bad, because it has so far affected his reason. But may it not be answered that a man might be altered by it *for the better*; that his spirits may be exhilarated without his reason being affected ...

I was agreeably disappointed in Sir Allan. He spoke warmly in favour of the Episcopal church, said his father had had a chaplain of the Church of England, and that the people chose to attend worship with him rather then go to the Presbyterian Kirk. Mr Johnson said they would all do so in the isles if they had an opportunity. Sir Allan agreed they would; and he said if he prevailed in his cause, he would build several chapels. We had our tea comfortably; and at night prayer books were brought. Miss MacLean read the evening service with a beautiful decency. We read the responses and other parts that congregations read. When she came to the prayer for the royal family she stopped. I bid her go to the prayer for the clergy. She did so. Mr Johnson pointed out to her prayers, which she read. After all, she and her sister sung the hymn on the Nativity of our Saviour. It was the nineteenth Sunday after Trinity. I shall remember it. Mr Johnson said it was most the agreeable Sunday evening he had ever passed in his life. We were all in good frame. I was truly pious.

I walked out in the dark to the cross, knelt before it, and holding it with both my hands, I prayed with strong devotion, while I had before me the image that my saviour died for the sins of the World. The sanctity of venerable Columba filled my imagination … I was for going into the chapel; but a tremor seized me for ghosts, and I hastened back to the house …

Sir Allan had made an apology at dinner that he had neither red wine nor biscuits, but that he expected both. Luckily the boat arrived with them this very afternoon. We had a couple of bottles of port and hard biscuits at night, after some roast potatoes, which is Sir Allan's simple fare by way of supper.

At breakfast I asked, 'What is the reason that we are angry at a traders opulence?'

'Why, sir,' said Mr Johnson, 'the reason is (though I don't undertake to prove there is a reason), we see no reasons in trade that should entitle a man to superiority. We are not angry at a soldier getting riches, because we see that he possesses qualities which we have not. If a man returns from battle, having lost one hand and the other full of gold, we feel he deserves the gold, but we cannot think that a fellow, by sitting all day at a desk, is entitled to get above us… A merchant may, perhaps, be a man of enlarged mind; but there is nothing in trade connected with an enlarged mind …

Young Coll told us he could run down a greyhound; 'For', he said, 'the dog runs himself out of breath by going too quick, then I get up with him and beat him at speed.' Mr Johnson observed that 'I explain the cause of this, by remarking that Coll had reason, and knew to moderate his pace, which the dog had not sense to know.' Indeed, Coll is not a philosopher. Mr Johnson said, 'He is a noble animal. He is as complete an islander as mortality can figure. He is a farmer, a sailor, a hunter, a fisher; he will run you down a dog. If any man has a tail, it is Coll. He is hospitable; and he has intrepidity of talk, whether he understands the subject or not.'

Tuesday 19th October. After breakfast we took leave of the young ladies, and of our excellent companion, Coll, to whom we had been so much obliged. He had now put us under the care of his chief, and was to hasten back to Skye. There was a kind of regret at parting with him which was both proper and pleasing. He had been a kind banker to me, in supplying me with silver ... Our rowers sung Erse songs, or rather howls. Sir Allan said the Indians in America sung in the same manner when rowing ... Mr Johnson said, 'This is rowing among the Hebrides, or nothing is ... '

That tells you much about Inchkenneth and the islands and things were very much the same in my time: the wheeled road up from the pier; visitors; family services; us out singing in the boat. Boswell goes on to write of how Coll was drowned the very next year in the Sound between Ulva and Mull. That's where Coll lived, on Ulva, the ancient seat of the MacQuarries, and there is an interesting piece in the book about the old *droits de signore* on that island. Boswell writes, 'Macguarie insisted that the *mercheth mulierum* "really did mean the privilege which a lord or a mayor or a baron, had to have the first night of all his vassals' wives" and that on Ulva, on the marriage of each of his tenants a sheep is due him, for which the compensation is fixed at five shillings ...' So you might say the goings on on the island in our time are not so unusual.

After Lady Redesdale died the island was sold to a doctor from London, Andrew Barlow and his wife Yvonne. He's the grandson of Charles Darwin, but we didn't get on. We left the island soon after the Barlows came. They had no idea of island life when they bought Inchkenneth. Friends of ours came down from Knock to picnic on the island. They left the boat on the shore. When they returned there was a drawing pin holding a note on the prow saying, 'Please, don't come back again'! After twenty years on the island, that came like a slap in the face. They didn't speak to us, they didn't approach the visitors, they crept up and left a note in the boat! That wasn't our way. That wasn't the Highland way of life; that wasn't island life. They're mellowing a bit now; they've settled in, but in those days they wanted the island all to themselves – and they had great plans for it – cattle, sheep – they were going to make a big commercial success of this and that, and there was no place for us in their plans. They wanted their own visitors. They bought up the houses and land on the Mull side, overlooking the island, to keep their privacy absolute. Now, we hear, they've handed the island on to their

daughter. She's a beadle down in Cambridge, the first woman beadle.

When we left Inchkenneth we went to a place called Ormsaig. It's halfway to Bunessan. That was for two or three years. It was only about twenty miles. Then we went to Rossal, by the Kinloch Hotel, where I did farm work. I was still very fit, but farmwork gets harder as you get older. Then I retired and we took this croft at the Aird of Kinloch. It's about sixty acres. I rented it then but after a few years we bought it. We bought it from the man Hickman, at the Kinloch Hotel. When he heard about the new legislation coming in, he tried to kick us out, but we were paying the rent. My rent was £50 a year and the new law was to give the crofters the right to buy their land at fifteen times the annual rent and he had no reason. Hickman tried to put the rent up to £300! We had a disagreement and finally it went to the Land Court. They fixed the rent at £75 and that suited us. We got this place for just over £1000. It's not like Inchkenneth – there's a lot of bog and a lot of stone – but it suits us. We built ourselves a new house and two of the boys, Robert and Kenneth, still live here with me. They've got caravans down by the shore.

Kenneth's a fencer – I'd say he's the best fencer on Mull. We now get a government subsidy and he's draining and dividing the land here. He works by himself. How he does it I don't know – every post stands solid as a rock, every key-post is capped with galvanised metal, turned and hammered like a work of art. They say you should live your life as though every day was your last, but farm as if you will live forever! Well, Kenneth does that, at least with his fences. I see them here for hundreds of years. He wasn't born in Inchkenneth – the nurse always took my wife across to Johnny Scott's cottage at Griben for a delivery – but he's named after Inchkenneth. Johnny Scott was a shepherd working for Lachlan MacLean at Knock farm.

Kenneth MacGillivray, the Aird of Kinloch, September 1999. (TN)

It's very important that we rejuvenate the land here because it's been in poor shape since the last century, when the men from Coll and Tiree would come here in boats to take back peat for fuel. Those islands are fertile but without peat, so they came here. Any ground not waterlogged was scalped down to rock and it takes a long time to recover. Life on Mull was rarely easy. The problems we've had in my lifetime are the same as Dr Johnson recognised when he passed through 230 years ago. Only in the last few years has the population been stabilised. This is what Johnson wrote:

> Some method to stop this epidemick desire of wandering, which spreads in contagion from valley to valley, deserves to be sought with great diligence. In more beautiful countries, the removal of one only makes room for the succession of another: but in the Hebrides, the loss of an inhabitant leaves a lasting vacuity; for nobody born in other parts of the

world will choose this country for his residence, and an island once depopulated will remain a desert, as long as the present facility of travel gives everyone, who is discontented and unsettled, the choice of his abode.

Let it be inquired, whether the first intention of those who are fluttering on the wing, and collecting a flock that they may take their flight, be to attain good, or to avoid evil. If they are dissatisfied with that part of the globe, which there birth has allotted them, and resolve not to live without the pleasures of happier climes; if they long for bright suns, and calm skies, and flowery fields, and fragrant gardens, I know not by what eloquence they can be persuaded, or by what offers they can be hired to stay.

But if they are driven from their native country by positive evils, and disgusted by ill-treatment, real or imaginary, it were fit to remove their grievances, and quiet their resentment; since, if they have been hitherto undutiful subjects, they will not much mend their principles by American conversations …

If the restitution of their arms will reconcile them to their country, let them have again those weapons, which will not be more mischievous at home than in the Colonies. That they may not fly from the increase of rent, I know not whether the general good does not require that the landlords be, for a time, restrained in their demands, and kept quiet by pensions proportionate to their loss.

To hinder resurrection by driving away the people, and to govern peaceably, by having no subjects, is an expedient that argues no great profundity of politicks. To soften the obdurate, to convince the mistaken, mollify the resentful, are worthy of a stateman; but it affords a legislator little self-applause to consider, that where there was formerly an insurrection, there is now a wilderness … The great business of insular policy now is to keep the people happy in their own country. As the world has been let in upon them, they have heard of happier climes, and less arbitrary government; and if they are disgusted, have emissaries amongst them ready to offer them land and houses, as a reward for deserting their clan and chief. Many have departed from the main of Scotland, and from the Island; and all that go may be considered lost as subjects to the British Crown; for a nation scattered in the boundless regions of America resembles rays diverging from a focus. All the rays remain, but the heat is gone. Their power consisted in their concentration: when they are dispersed, they have little effect.

It may be thought they are happier by the change; but they

Neil and Kenneth MacGillivray,
the Aird of Kinloch, 1999.
(TN)

are not happy as a nation, for they are a nation no longer.

There are some however who think this emigration has raised terrour disproportionate to its real evil; and that it is only a new mode of doing what was always done. The Highlands, they say, never maintained their natural inhabitants; but the people, when they found themselves too numerous, instead of extending cultivation, provided for themselves by a more compendious method; and sought better fortune in other countries. But they did not go away in collective bodies; but withdrew invisibly, a few at a time; but the whole number of fugitives was not less, and the difference between the other times and this, is only the same as between evaporation and effusion.

This is plausible, but I am afraid it is not true. Those who went before, if they were not sensibly missed, as the argument supposes, must have gone either in less number, or in a manner less detrimental, than at present; because formerly there was no complaint. Those who then left the country were generally the idle dependants on overburdened families; or men who had no property; and therefore carried away only themselves. In the present eagerness of emigration, families, and almost communities go away together. Those who were considered as prosperous and wealthy sell their stock and carry away the money. Once none went away but the useless and poor; in some parts there is now reason to fear, that none will stay but those who are too poor to remove themselves, and too useless to be removed at the cost of others.

I don't agree with all of that but the picture Dr Johnson paints was true for our family. We all went off to Australia. Things were very hard in the 'fifties. I was paid £3 a week. We had the bungalow. We had meat, grain, vegetables, but it was hard to see a good future for the children here in those days. We went away – but then we came back and we don't regret that. Things weren't great for us in Australia: Netta's health was bad and Lady Anne was wanting us back. So, in the end, we came and we settled back into Inchkenneth as though we'd never left it. My wages went up; the children did well at school; life was good. We enjoyed the winters on our own and we enjoyed the visitors in the summer. Lady Anne used to say, 'It's nice to see them come but it's also nice to see them go,' and we thought the same. When she died, she left us two sets of coronation chairs. The chairs she and her husband had sat on for the crowning of King George V and King George VI in Westminster Abbey. We still have them, through there. They were made in High Wycombe. The George V chairs are in the Chippendale, classical style. They're made of beech but stained dark brown. The George VI chairs are made of oak, stained slightly silver. They're quite simple, half modern, half medieval and all have a little metal holder for your prayer book.

Well that was it. The Redesdales sold up, the Barlows came in, and we were away. Lachie Knock – Lachie MacLean – he has the Knock farm. He keeps his sheep in Inchkenneth. He and his wife, Chrissie, they get on well with the Barlows – you should speak to him about how things are on Inchkenneth today.

Lachlan MacLean

KNOCK, MULL

'Introducing themselves, they would always say, "MacPhail of the Glen."'

Our MacLeans were never adventurous with names. My father was Donald, I'm Lachlan, my eldest son is Lachlan, my second son is Donald – that's how it goes, forward and backwards, over the generations. The postman causes trouble here most mornings! Mull was, for centuries, a MacLean island, but there's few enough of us these days. However, we're here and the clan chief is at Duart Castle. Between the two of us, we manage to keep a grip.

I was born here on Mull, but my father and mother came from Skye. They met by a circuitous route. She went down to Manchester to work. My father followed his sister out to Montana. He went as a shepherd, sheep-ranching on horseback. That was about 1910. He enjoyed the life very much and when his sister died, the family out there took him in. Being in the States he missed the Great War. There were many Highland shepherds in Montana. In 1922 he returned to get married. The plan was to go back after the children had been educated here, after we'd learned Gaelic. Both my parents were native Gaelic speakers. It turned out I was an only child – but my father still didn't trust the American education system! He thought it was too close to brain-washing, though that term was not invented in those days. He wanted to root me here in Scotland before going back to Montana but, in the end, that never happened. He settled down in Mull, the Second World War came, he took Knock farm and our fate was decided. He ran Knock and I ran Glen More. We came in here fifty-two years ago. When he died I took over both leases. Later on I was able to buy eighty acres of arable ground, next door here, over the bridge. So that's me. With the two boys I run 30,000 acres. Ten thousand we rent ourselves and on the rest we run sheep for others.

Opposite.
Lachlan MacLean of Knock Farm,
Isle of Mull, 1999 (TN)

Knock Farm, home to Lachlan MacLean for fifty-two years, 1999. (TN)

For fifty years our landlord was Lord Mazarine — that's an Irish title. He lived most of the year down in Kent. Now he's sold up and this place has been bought by a Belgian, a man called Delwart. He has another place, I believe, at Knoydart. What he'll do with us is still to be decided. Lord Mazarine was, I would say, a neutral force here on Mull. He never bothered us and we never bothered him. But in our time, over fifty years, he made no improvements at all. If we wanted improvements we had to do them, and pay for them, ourselves. But, we like the old ways, so that didn't bother us too much. Look at the house here: we've always said we'd do it up, but we like it the way it is so why change it? There's many an ugly bungalow sprung up in the Highlands since we did nothing to this place! This house has been lived in for hundreds of years. It's a wee bit run down but you can feel the character of the place, we feel we know the people who lived here before us — and it's not in me to change things for the worse.

Knock Farm. The name comes from the Gaelic, *cnoc*, meaning a knoll or hillock, a rise of ground. The Knock steadings stand to the west of the Oyster Park — that's the big flat field at the head of Loch na Keal. There are three prehistoric graveyards here, there are standing stones, many remnants of ancient settlements. Even the trees, over the burn here, are very old. Great beeches and oaks. The ground is undisturbed and the chanterelles come up year after year. It was at the Oyster Park that the Clan MacLean gathered. They gathered there to go to Bannockburn; they gathered there to go to Flodden, to Inverkeithing; they gathered there for the 'Fifteen Rebellion. This is an ancient place, steeped in history. It's where the River Forsa runs into the sea. Behind us, the glen leads up to a very narrow pass which can be defended by just a few dozen men, like the Pass of Thermopylae. I'm not saying we could hold it against NATO, or sustained attach by Cruise missiles but, in the old days, we could hold back an army – on foot, or mounted – and stop all passage of guns and equipment. So, we MacLeans have returned and we're in here yet.

There's a story about Lord Mazarine boarding the ferry at Craignure. He arrived there with a large number of cases. One of the deckhands, Alec MacLachlan, carried them aboard and stacked them away. He made several journeys. When he came back down the gangplank for the last time, Lord Mazarine was still talking to a friend on the pier. Alec stood there, about four yards away, and Lord Mazarine said, 'I expecth you'we waithing fwor a twip.' This would be back in the early 'sixties. He had a speech impediment. Alec didn't say anything but stood his ground. Then Lord Mazarine sought in his pocket and handed over a sixpence. That would be worth about four pence today. Well, Alec MacLachlan looked at Lord Mazarine and he put the sixpence on his thumb and tossed it in the air. He let it land on the pier and roll to a stop. 'There you are, sir,' he said, 'if you're ever short of a sixpence, ye'll know where to find it. You know what I mean!' He added that – and he turned on his heel. Lord Mazarine bumbled, 'The man's an oaf,' and went up the plank. The word 'oaf' came naturally to him. Alec MacLachlan let things rest there but you can see how insults fester into long running sores. All ranks like to be treated properly in the Highlands.

But, ourselves, we never had a serious disagreement with Lord Mazarine. We rent 10,000 acres and we looked after 1000 head of sheep on his ground. That's a service we give against the rental here. Delwart has not yet decided what he's going to do with his estate. He's got a young factor in Edinburgh. He's the one I'm worried about. It's his first job and he wants to make his mark, but he doesn't know this part of the world. It would do him good to sit down and listen to the people who know farming here. I'd like him to take his time, get things right and not blunder about like so many before him. I'm seventy-six now, my boys are forty and thirty-eight. They work every hour the Lord gives them. We know the ground – I hope He'll listen to us. I don't think there'll be another generation willing to work the way my boys work. It's not just the day-to-day slog across 30,000 acres of mountain, but all the paperwork and restrictions. I've got Parkinson's disease, but it's not myself, it's them, I worry about – it's the boys. There are so many hoops they're forced to jump through. For instance, because we get subsidies from the EU, we have to be ready to have our sheep counted by the Department of Agriculture at any time. If you keep sheep in a field in Belgium, it's not difficult to count them, but if you keep 3000

sheep spread over four mountains, it's not easy, it's expensive and it can be dangerous. We, normally, will lose about twenty per counting, in rock-falls and bogs, bringing them down. It might take up to a week to get all of them in. The Department boys try to be helpful but the ewes get distressed, the lambs get lost – all for nothing but to show you're not cheating with numbers!

We have twenty dogs but more and more we depend on CBs nowadays. I stand at the bottom, or move round in the Landrover, directing operations – relaying where the sheep are. Sometimes we get help in from neighbours and we have one boy lives in, Norman MacPhail. When his mother died, he moved in with us and he's like one of the family. He's a wee bit wild and he loves cars – it's autosport every weekend! But he's a great worker. I can't find fault with youngsters today, not out here in the islands. The only thing is they all rush, they all work too hard. In the old days bringing the sheep down you'd wander back and forth over the hill till you met the next man. Then you'd have blether and set off again. The day might be long but the pace was slow and you had company even on the highest reaches. Now it's a race from morning to night. Donald – that's my eldest boy – he's up before six and it'll be a rare day he finishes the paperwork before midnight. You have to keep abreast of it every day or you're lost. My daughter runs the medical practice for the doctors in Oban. She comes over at weekends to check everything off on the computers. It's all go.

Donald's on a lot of committees; island committees, agriculture committees; he's a judge at the Dalmally Show. He's no time for anything but work, no time to look for a wife! Lachlan – he's got two children, Gaelic speakers. They don't speak Gaelic at home but they've gone into the Gaelic immersion classes at school and done very well. They come home to speak Gaelic to their old grandad, and I enjoy that very much. Whether they'll ever want to follow our footsteps here, working the farm, I more and more doubt. They'd do better taking up golf. Maybe they should buy Inchkenneth and turn it into a golf course with a helicopter pad and a grand restaurant. Money furnishes the best of tables, as though by magic! And we sell good lambs for the price of a dram.

We still keep a few head of cattle out on Inchkenneth and a few dozen sheep. We've had them there for twenty years. They keep the grass down. It suits the Barlows and it suits us. It's a marvellous little island. We like to go out. We also used to run Aorsa, for Lord Mazarine. That's the other island in Loch na Keal. It's more rocky and less fertile and in the end it wasn't worth the bother. It's been uninhabited for years but we like to keep an eye on Inchkenneth. It's the only boat work we do. It makes a change. We've always kept our own boat down there, but the Barlows now have a landing craft; if we get the use of that, everything's easy. Up until seven years ago we still used to drive cattle to and from Inchkenneth. If we did that today we'd have to do it by night – there are so

Opposite.
Lachlan MacLean looking for the
Rock of the Sword at Leac an Li.
(TN)

Loch na Keal, looking west towards the cliffs of Griben, 1999. (TN)

many tourists passing that the Animal Rights people would be on us like a ton of bricks. We used to enjoy the droving, herding them forward with rubber dinghies. You have to be right there on the backs on the animals, driving them forward, keeping them walking the ridge of the sandbank and not taking a shortcut through the deep water. You needed a good calm day.

Horses would swim out to Inchkenneth on a rope, behind the boat. They were used for ploughing and harvesting. In the old days, the nuns used to send their grain to Iona. In fact they used to farm most of the good ground on this side as well. It was known as 'The Black Woman's Land'. That described the prioress in her black habit. There is good land on Mull but not much. Sorley MacLean, the poet, whom I used to know quite well, liked to speak about 'Great Mull of the Trees', but if that wasn't his invention, it must have been a very ancient saying indeed because even in the old poems where we have men going away to battle, it's never the trees that they mention, it's 'the misty hills'. Those are the words that describe this place in historical memory, and the same is true of Skye. But in the bogs here you do find the stumps of great trees preserved and they must have imposed themselves on the minds of the early peoples and perhaps this got into their earliest songs, or maybe it was Sorley himself made the connection. There was a battle here at Knock called the Battle of the Leafy-Boughed Nose and Glen Forsa is certainly well forested today.

Clan MacLean power, here in Mull, here at Knock, goes back before the Battle of Largs in 1266. They supported King Alexander against the Vikings,

The great beach trees behind the walled garden at Knock, 1999. (TN)

and as a reward they got additional lands. But it was later that the big endowment came – when one of the MacLean chiefs married a daughter of the Lord of the Isles, and her dowry consisted of great tracts of land right down as far as Jura. At least that was the understanding of the old men here, when I was young. We had just a few of the old *seanachies*, the old historians, left. Everything came down by way of mouth, but it was all very well organised and they would take you back hundreds of years – to the 'Forty-five, to Inverkeithing, to Bannockburn. There was a shepherd here, Hugh MacNeilage – that's a very old Mull name – he lived up Glen Forsa and worked for the Gardynes at Ghodail. He was a man with a great memory for facts and history and song. It all came down by word of mouth, not from books or written history. My father had the farm in Glen Forsa and I used to go up to see Hugh. His wife was a wonderful cook and he spoke nothing but Gaelic. He was a quiet man and slow to start. He was tall and very thin and even in his eighties he had the caste of youth still on him. He never seemed to age. There were many things he would say in Gaelic that he would never think to say in English. It was as though he had a secret knowledge that only existed in Gaelic and which he could only reveal to those whom he trusted and knew the language. The language was the key to something beyond the language.

Well, Hugh MacNeilage was a great influence on my youth. He would speak about the Battle of Largs as though it happened last week and he had a strange way of cross-referencing his historical remembrances with songs. He was very musical and he played the accordion. He told me so many things.

The MacLean's Highland ponies grazing above Loch na Keal. The island of Ulva, back left, 1999. (TN)

Unfortunately, most of them I now forget. I wish I'd written them down or set my mind to remembering Hugh's own version of history. His songs were great; many were local to the glen and most I never heard sung by anyone else. But the trouble was that I had to work. I was busy then – as the boys are now. He had, himself, two boys and a girl, but they didn't seem interested in his *bardachd* and all are now dead, anyway. He was a man of the glen, but he'd also worked on Ulva and knew all parts of Mull, so, in losing him, Mull lost something irrecoverable. He died in about 1956 and most of all he had went with him to the grave. It's a tragedy.

In fact, you could say, it was a double tragedy because there was another man involved, a Dr Gray. He was brother to Pipe Major William Gray. He was an ear, nose and throat surgeon in Glasgow, married to a woman from Iona, and he made a great collection of the history and folklore of the island of Mull. He knew Gaelic and he knew Hugh MacNeilage. He was a brilliant man, but his fuse was short and his pride great. And that fact was to prove our undoing. Because he spent a lot of time on Mull, he was appointed to what was called the Council of Social Services. I was on the same committee, representing Salen. There were representatives from every part of Mull. I knew Dr Gray quite well and one day he came to a meeting with this big book, this great folder of papers, under his arm. He told me it was the full history of the island: Glen Forsa, Glen Candle, Tobermory, Iona, Hugh MacNeilage – everything, and he was going to present it to the council, for the island. Well, the meeting started and there was various business discussed. Then, announcing A.O.R.B., the chairman informed us that two old ladies – the two Miss Turners – had written a short, anecdotal history of Mull. He said he'd enjoyed it so much that he would like to recommend that the council support it for publication, etc. Of course, the council members were delighted and roundly commended the two ladies' history ... Well, that did it – how could Dr Gray step in and offer his own work after that? If the Social Services Council was willing to subsidise silly sentimental nonsense they were not worthy of what he brought. He put his hand over this folder and took it down into his lap. Instead of announcing the handing over of that unique, historic document, he said not a word and went home. Later he told me, 'If that's what they want, they won't have wanted what I've got!' He said he would burn every word he'd written. Now, I don't know whether he carried out his threat or whether he hid his manuscripts, or gifted them in his will, but, if they exist, I'm certain they'd be of enormous value to Mull today, and honour the memory of Hugh MacNeilage as well.

Sorley MacLean first came to Mull in 1938. He was English teacher at Tobermory School. He didn't teach me because I was already at Oban, but we knew about him. It seems that, for personal reasons, he didn't enjoy the year he spent here, but when he was retired he used to like coming. He would give lectures on peculiar subjects, like 'The MacLean Skull'! I used to wonder why he would look at me – in such a way! Many of his Mull poems are sad poems; these are two verses I remember:

> *Tha larach eaglais 'san Ros Mhuileach*
> *Anns nach robh luchd-eisdeachd*
> *No seirbhis crabhaidh o'n latha*
> *A chuireadh Inbhir-Cheitein.*
>
> *Latha 'n tug uabhar ar cinnidh*
> *An leum ard anns a' bhiothbhuan,*
> *An cruin-leum a rinn am milleadh,*
> *A dh' fhag an darach 'na chritheann ...*

> There is the ruin of a church in the Ross of Mull
> In which there has not been a congregation
> Or a religious service since the day
> Inverkeithing was fought.
>
> The day when the pride of our clan
> Took the high jump into the permanent;
> The standing jump that spoiled them
> That left their oak an aspen.

Sorley was appointed bard to Clan MacLean. He was a socialist, and the old clan system had a strong socialist basis to it. Everybody kept in contact and everybody helped each other. There was one hereditary chief but, beyond that, everything was held in common, with everyone bearing their responsibilities and particular authority – a herd, a boatman, a smith would have a very real authority. Things were held and treated in common. The stronger would help the weaker. People with a poor harvest here would be helped by those having a good harvest there. Although the Highlands were always relatively barren, the population was thinly spread and there was rarely a shortage of protein. We had cattle, horses, goats, sheep, pigs, plenty of wild fowl, venison, seabirds, fish, plenty of shellfish. There would be times of hardship, but famine was unheard of in the old days. Water in the mountains is good – and we knew how to make whisky! Even today there are still two beautiful wells high up on Ben More. They're fenced off to keep the water pure and the boys drink from them when they're up gathering sheep. The old summer sheilings lie below them. One is called 'the Scourie', but the other seems to have lost its name. Sorley wrote beautiful poems about wells.

> At the edge of a mountain there is a green nook
> Where the deer eat water-cress,
> In its side a great unruffled eye of water,
> A shapely jewel-like spring …

Although the MacLeans married into the Lords of the Isles there could still be trouble between the MacLeans and the MacDonalds. In 1586 an army of 2500 MacDonalds landed just down the coast here. They came up to Knock and they went into Glen Candle, which was where the women, the children and cattle were taken for safety. It can be, as I said, defended by just a very few men. So MacLean sent a scouting vanguard under the command of his son to check out how things were. He was either over-confident or over-zealous, for the whole vanguard was surrounded and wiped out. Well-pleased with their work, the MacDonalds went back down the side of Loch na Keal after cattle. The MacLeans bade their time, then gathered at a place called Lech Lee, where every man ran his sword across a rock which was believed to have magic powers and healing properties. The rock and the sword groove are there to this day. It was Hugh MacNeilage who first showed it to me. Well, after the ritual sword sharpening at Lech Lee, the MacLeans mounted their own surprise attack and it was a great success. Huge losses were inflicted on the MacDonalds and they had to escape by sea as best they could. All the rocks up there are scarred by glaciation, so it's not easy to find the sword 'groove' – unless you know the place well.

The population of Mull reached about 10,000 during the

Napoleonic Wars. That's the official figure and that's said to be the maximum we reached, but Hugh MacNeilage and other old people here told me the real figures were a good deal higher. Today, with Social Security and Income Support, and threats of imprisonment, it's in the interest of the poorer families to declare every member of a household. But 200 years ago many people had good reason to keep quiet about numbers, and there was very little anybody could do about it. People became invisible because rents might be increased. Whole villages could be declared over-populated and cleared. There would be men who wouldn't want to be taken off into the army or navy; there would be tinkers and others still living rough in the woods; run-away women. Mull was a wild place – so the real population might have been at least 12,000. It was a combination of war, over-population, the decline of the kelp industry and the coming of the big sheep flocks that precipitated a rapid decline in the population. There's a story that, in 1815, men returning from Waterloo came back to their village, up the glen here, and found the whole place deserted. Every single person gone. That was at the head of Glen Forsa. That was a place from which many of the oldest inhabitants of Mull originally came. There were just two names in that village, MacGillivray and MacPhail. The MacGillivrays were hereditary bowmen to the

Sorley MacLean (back left), 1937, photographed with staff at Portree High School – the year before he moved to Mull. His great friend Jack Stewart, with whom he planned to go to Spain to fight in the Spanish Civil War, is at the back, far right. (RM)

Lachie MacLean traces the sword grooves used to ritually sharpen the dirks and swords of Clan MacLean before the Battle of Leac an Li. (TN)

MacLean chief at Duart Castle and they gained rights to the lands around the village and, because they were bowmen, many of them changed their name to Fletcher. That put a third name into the head of Glen Forsa. Our boy here, Norman MacPhail – he can trace his people back more than 1000 years. Introducing themselves, the MacPhails, when I was young, would always say, 'MacPhail of the Glen'.

We're not heavy drinkers at Knock but drink has been a problem for some in the Highlands. Not so long ago there was a farmer here, getting old, with no descendants – so, one night, he was saying in the pub that he'd give away his farm, 'tomorrow, if I met a man would treasure it'. There was a shepherd there and he replied, 'I'd give my right arm to go into a farm and know I was my own master.' Well, it wasn't rhetoric the farmer spoke and within hours the deal was done. The shepherd would have the farm and everything on it. The only thing the old man kept for himself was the right to live in the house till his death.

That shepherd was a Lewisman and he was a beautiful singer. He moved into the bothy with his wife and his family. He worked very hard and things went very well till, quite suddenly, his health went down. They had worries about money and he thought he had cancer. He started to drink to assuage the pain and he drank too much. However, he was lucky – he was in Glasgow when an ulcer burst in his stomach. He was operated on, he got better, and was put in a clinic where he was weaned off the booze. He came back to Mull on the wagon.

I told you, that man was a beautiful singer – in fact he was a cousin of Calum Kennedy's – and when he'd had a few drams he would sing all night. But, coming back to Mull, knowing he had to abstain from alcohol, he stopped going out and he didn't sing – until one night. I can still see it, clear as day. There was a do here, for the farmers and shepherds, and he was asked to sing. He refused. I remember there was a glass of orange juice on the table before him. He didn't want to sing and for a second time he refused. But when he was asked for a third time his wife passed him a big tumbler with a clear liquid in it. He picked it up, looked at it, and drank in a oner, then he rose and stared to sing. He sang beautiful songs as though he'd never been away. There was an ecstasy about him! But that clear liquid must have been gin or vodka and, within an hour, that man was all-over-the-shop; within two hours he was paralytic and he had to be carried home. Within a year he was out of the farm.

I've always wondered why his wife did that. Did she forget? Did she so much want to hear him sing? She wasn't drunk herself. Did she want to bring him down? We'll never know. That was thirty years ago but I remember that story for two reasons. First because it's a story human of goodness and folly and second because it tells you something about farming. You have to have the wherewithal, you have to have the money and you have to have discipline. So much money is spent up-front in farming, and most of your money comes in just once a year – after the big sales. It's dedicated, round-the-clock work and you need to be born to it. People will have to trust you and the bank manager will have to trust you. We had a great bank manager here. Angus Macintyre at Tobermory. He'd phone me up around midnight and ask me up for a chat, all Gaelic. Two or three hours and then I'd drive home. I'd say that man did more for the economy of Mull than every Enterprise Board in history! His son was Kenny Macintyre, the broadcaster, who died just recently. We like the human touch out here.

We had a shepherd, Johnny Scott, a great man and a great character. He lived down at Griben, opposite Inchkenneth. He was shepherd there for over thirty years. He was a man liked a drink – but it was always weekends and he kept it under control, until he retired. Now he's moved away up to Salen and drink runs his life. But he was a very brilliant man and a very interesting man. It was in his cottage the children from Inchkenneth were born. When Neil MacGillivray was boatman there, he'd always bring his wife over to Johnny's place for the birth of all their children. Johnny speaks Gaelic, English, Italian and German. He was a prison guard during the war and found he had this gift for languages. He just picked them up – from the prisoners – and very soon he got given a job as an official interpreter. When the war ended he should have gone off to university or become a businessman but he came back to Mull to work as shepherd down at Griben.

Johnny Scott was a generous man. My wife, Chrissie, still goes up to see him at Salen, but he's unshaven now and nobody wants to know him after two in the afternoon. He's like the Cyclops: everybody wants to keep out of his way! One day my son Donald had to drive him home after a heavy night's drinking, and Donald was put out and bad tempered about it. When they got to Griben, Johnny asked him to wait whilst he went into the house – it's right there on the shore – and Johnny came back with a parcel all neatly tied with string. Inside was a beautiful pair of binoculars. It was a present, for next day it was Donald's twenty-first birthday! You can imagine what Donald thought of his bad temper then.

That was the kind of man Johnny Scott was and is yet, despite the drink. He's like Socrates was: 'nothing much to look at exteriorly but garment to the bravest spirit' and a notable intellect. When we did pony trekking here, he used to help out. One fortnight there was an Italian count staying on holiday in the big house. After Johnny had saddled the ponies up, he was listening to the count talking to his children. Suddenly he was talking about Johnny and Johnny didn't like what he was hearing. He let him go on for a moment, then he shouted, 'Avanti Mussolini!' And, in perfect Italian, he dressed that man down, right there in front of his children! He told him he's spent three years of his life trying to get Italian Fascist prisoners-of-war to see the light of our common humanity! And he wasn't going to take insults, nor be treated like an ignorant peasant by anyone, be he a count or be he a fool! It was a devastating attack but well justified. It was the perfect Italian that was the *coup de grâce*, and the count apologised! In fact he broke into tears, for he knew he'd done wrong. There is a divinity in anger sometimes, and that was one time. It was like Christ throwing the money-changers out of the Temple.

Now he wanders drunk around Salen, unshaven. He should have been more fully stretched than he ever was, once the war was over, but, then again, why should there not be intelligent men working here, wearing clothes suitable for hard work? Why not?

Many was the time we drove sheep and cattle up to Salen market or for shipment to Oban. It would be a big job getting the young cattle away from their mothers. As wild as deer they'd be, after a summer loose on the hill. We'd go up the day before loading, pen them in a neighbour's field and stay the night. Then we'd drive them aboard up a great plank gangway. On a rough crossing things would get pretty messy with the beasts just loose-penned and sliding about. I remember October 1939. We were waiting at Croggan pier and we had to wait all day. The ship didn't come in till eight o'clock and we had to load in the dark. It was a night of squalls and high seas and, of course, we came into Oban in 'blackout'. I was the youngest of the drovers there and it fell to me to count the beasts as they came off. In fact I had to, because all the older men had spent the

day in the pub and were well past counting cattle stampeding off a boat into pitch-blackness.

Well, I knew we had ninety-seven cattle on board, but I'd only got to ninety-six when the gangway fell silent! It was no moment to quibble! 'All off!' I shouted and raced after the herd into the darkness, and above the shouts and bellows I could hear great splashes as the beasts round the edges plunged into the harbour! But the mass kept going – and those in the water started swimming – trying to keep up with the herd bellowing above them – and they all scrambled out at the shore to rejoin the main party! The whole herd then pattered and roared its way through Oban, just as the pubs were closing their doors! In total blackness, the rain lashing down, all hell was let loose! That herd scoured Oban like a river in flood. It was like the bull-running in Pamplona! The market was down by the railway station. Once they were penned, we got permission to put on the lights for just long enough to check what had arrived. Ninety-seven cattle all in regular order! It was a miracle! Ninety-seven cattle and eight of the Oban folk who'd got caught in the flood, mostly drunks! As the lights were switched off, a policeman arrived shouting, 'There's been a complaint!' Then he told us it was illegal to drive cattle at night without lights! But what else could we do? One of the old Mull men shouted, 'You show us the place to stick a light in a bullock and we'll light up the lot of them!' The only place we could find would have doubled their speed and set Oban on fire! A great laugh we had as we dried out by a fire with a dram and a half.

Lachlan Maclean at Leac an Li above Loch na Keal, typical Mull sheep country and site of the battle between MacLeans and MacDonalds in 1586.
(TN)

Every autumn you'd get 8000 head of the cattle gathered there in Oban. It was a great sight to see and all night the trains would be leaving full-laden with the beasts all lowing and their horns sticking up in the moonlight. That went right on till 1954 –55. Oban was the collecting point for all the cattle from Uist, Tiree, Coll, Iona, Mull and much of the north of Argyll. The tourists would mostly be away by October and the weather was usually poor. The cattle were still horned in those days. It was a real Wild West experience. My father said he saw nothing in Montana that was wilder than the sight of the Oban police trying to tie red lamps to the tails of a herd of stirks at full gallop!

Sheep are easier to move than cattle in a town, but whereas it's the young cattle that cause trouble amongst the beasts, it's the old ewes – the cast ewes – that are the troublemakers amongst sheep. If they came off a boat after rain and there were puddles and standing water in the streets, you knew you were in for fireworks! Sheep are very susceptible to reflections and shadows. In Australia they leap over the shadows of trees as though every one was a five-bar gate; in Oban they jump onto car-bonnets and into Kennedy's Tea-rooms! I've seen a ram challenge himself outside a barber's shop and go right through the window! I was once staying in a bed-and-breakfast house when a half dozen ewes came bounding up the stairs! It was lucky I was there. They didn't need a circus in Oban when the sales were on! People got bitten by dogs and shat on by cows! But the wonderful thing was in those days almost no one complained. It was all part of life. It was what life was. Nowadays there'd be court cases, compensation claims, a permanent team of stress counsellors on standby – every time a cattle boat came in from Mull.

My father lost an eye to a horn. So you won't be surprised to hear that as soon as dehorning came in we dehorned every beast we had. It made everything easier. Today we just have two horned Highlands, they look nice and the tourists take photographs of them. Two injections were given to the calves, one to numb the pain and the other to inhibit the growth of the horn. I still prefer the beef of the Highland to anything else – it's a beautiful marbled flesh, very succulent – but the market for Highlands has been bad for several seasons and we now farm Luing cattle. I'm not so keen on the Limousin or the big continentals. Everything changes – nothing changes. Just today, 28th October 1999, my two boys have taken two lorry loads of cast ewes to Oban. We can't keep them, we can't sell them, so the choice was to shoot them and burn them or give them away. The boys refuse to shoot them, so they've taken them on floats to Oban to give to a man in the Lowlands who's got space for 2000 head. They're doing that at their own expense; they won't get a penny for those ewes. In good grass and with feeding those sheep will raise another two or three lambs, but up here, they're finished. We can't sell them for meat, so what do we do? With whole

nations said to be starving you have to wonder what's going on in the world. If we let nature take its course and left them to die on the hill, we'd be liable to prosecution. Even if they were pecked white-clean by eagles, we'd be for it.

We've got plenty of sea-eagles on Mull, they were reintroduced to Rum and have spread. Some people call them 'the flying door', they're so big and broad in the wing. We're glad they're back but the RSPB boys seem to be overdoing it on Mull. Tamper with one thing and you affect another. We hardly see a golden eagle now. Donald found a beautiful golden eagle – with its crop slashed open. The sea-eagle is a much heavier bird than the golden eagle, so the golden, if it's in anything less than prime condition, will go down before it. We took the slashed eagle over to the RSPB. Its wing was damaged, but whether the wing was damaged before the sea-eagles went for it, or whether they damaged it, we'll never know. It died anyway.

Bird watching is a big business these days. Huge numbers of what they call 'twitchers' come up around Eastertime to join our friendly Neighbourhood Watch on the sea-eagle eyries. This year we had four policemen specially drafted in from Glasgow to keep guard. They all stayed in the Isle of Mull Hotel, at £50 a night! It was a great holiday in the Highlands for them. Now it seems some of those egg-collectors have turned collecting into a sport – a game with the authorities – so the big fines they're giving out just increase the gamble. They've put video cameras on the ferries to keep watch for known villains. Its great publicity for the RSPB – they're rolling in money! But for us, working the hills, we just get trampers disturbing the sheep and enough questions to drive you to silence – or drink! We pretend we know nothing.

The raven is another protected bird whose numbers have soared. There is a fine strong bird. Years ago we would lose two or three lambs to the ravens. They tear the tongues out of the living lambs. We get compensation for every skinned or disembowelled lamb we can prove killed by a raven, but it's not easy to find the skin of a lamb on a mountain. If we kept our sheep in a paddock, or zoo, things might be easier. We could claim compensation and throw the skins to the wolves and the foxes! Twenty pounds a unit is what we get paid, but what makes a unit I've forgotten! All I know is there was a man last year brought in three skins he'd found and got nothing, because three lambs didn't make a unit – so he didn't even make the starting gate! The small man and the hill men are at a disadvantage when it comes to fulfilling their units.

We don't do the pony-trekking any longer – we just let our ponies wander the hill. There's been a great growth of interest in horses in many parts but we don't have the time to organise things now. We've thought about selling, but the prices are so low that with transportation costs the prices we'd get would never cover the cost of shipment, so we just leave our ponies out on the hill to enjoy their lives, their freedom. Highlands they are. That was my wife Chrissie's special interest but, like me, she's getting older and she now finds the dogs quite enough. It costs her over £200 a month to feed our twenty dogs. Four of them are retired, but for us, for the wicked, there is no rest! Like the foxes, the little foxes, there is no place where the hill farmer can rest his head. I jest, but it's true!

I jest. When you're born to farming you enjoy it; you know nothing else. Farming ties you to the land and the land ties you to history, especially if your family has long association with a place, as ours does. When you stand here above the Oyster Park, or when you're down on Inchkenneth and you look west to Iona and east to Knock, you feel 2000 years to be a very short span. And you need not feel cut off from the world of ideas – unless you want to be. We have our books, we have the television and wireless, and with the new ferries we can be in Oban in little less than an hour. Writers and artists still go over to Inchkenneth to work as they did in the time of Sir Allan MacLean, the Mitfords, the time of Columba. Not long ago they made a film on Inchkenneth, *Walk me Home* it was called. We were called in to help out.

The writer of the film was a man called John Berger. He won the Booker Prize in 1972. That was for a novel called *G*, and he did a big series on television called *Ways of Seeing*. He quite often goes out to Inchkenneth. He's an old friend of the Barlows. Yvonne Barlow has lent me his books, but, I have to say, I've never found them easy going. He stayed there for weeks to write a play called *Goya's Last Portrait*. That was a joint project with a French writer called Nella Bielski. When they came to do the filming, they wanted sheep in the old ruined chapel for one of the scenes, so I went over with Donald and two of the dogs to put the sheep where they wanted. It was a beautiful day. The cameraman was a Russian called Vadim Youssof. The chief actress was a German called Angela Winckler, and Berger wasn't just the main writer he was the lead actor as well. It was a love story with the two of them – they weren't young – going away upstairs to the big four-poster bed.

I never saw the film they made, but our little corner of the world still makes its mark, as it has over the centuries – from Lindisfarne to Montana to Hollywood. One of the people who worked on that film was telling me that Inchkenneth played a big part in the idea behind *The English Patient*. That was the film that won all the Oscars. It was based on a novel by a friend of John Berger's called Michael Ondaatje and it seems he got many of his ideas via Berger and his knowledge of the history of Inchkenneth. The main character in *The English Patient*, the burnt airman, was based on the character of Count Almasy, an Austro-Hungarian aristocrat who was the lover of Unity Mitford who, as you know, lived many years 'marooned' and disabled on Inchkenneth. And if you study the story of *The English Patient*, both as a novel and as a film, you'll find it a Second World

This page top.
Film crew in front of Inchkenneth
House, 1992. Cameraman Vadim
Youssof (framed by the house) was
Tarkowsky's cameraman for the
film Andrew Rublyov, *recently*
described as the greatest film
ever made. (AW)

This page, bottom.
Vadim Youssof rehearses a move for
the film Walk Me Home *in front*
of the ruined bungalow in which
Neil MacGillivray once lived with
his family. Inchkenneth, 1992.
(AW)

Opposite top.
Inchkenneth, looking west past 'The
Humpies' to the distant outline of
Iona. The actor, John Berger, gathers
oysters in the bay, 1992.
(AW)

Opposite bottom.
John Berger as 'William' in
Walk Me Home, *Inchkenneth,*
1992. (AW)

War version of Berger's First World War story, *G. The English Patient* is full of the most amazing connections between the life of Unity Mitford and Scotland's historical contact with North Africa and Italy: empires, crashed aeroplanes, subterfuge, sexual love, the need for the kind of communal experience we once had here – they're all there. For instance, there was a tinker piper from Kintyre, his name was Jock Townsley. He was out on the Anzio Beachhead with the Argyll and Sutherland Highlanders in 1944. Under heavy enemy fire he suddenly broke cover and ran from foxhole to foxhole calling out, 'Is there anybody here from Campbeltown?' In extremis he wanted to be with someone from home. That

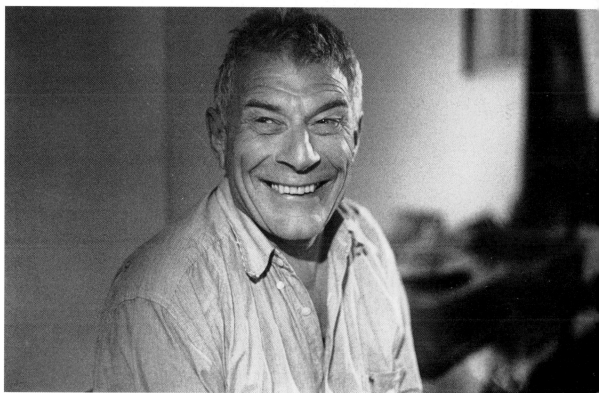

story was told by the pipe major of the Campbeltown Pipe Band and passed on to John Berger … And, on the train, at the start of *The English Patient*, as the war in Italy draws towards its close, a dying Canadian soldier cries out to one of the nurses, 'Is there anybody here from Picton?' The idea is exactly the same.

Now it may be chance that made Ondaatje decide his dying soldier should say that, or synchronicity, but it's more likely that the tale that went with Berger from Scotland went on to Ondaatje – and on to Hollywood. That's the way the things are – but nobody, looking at that film, *The English Patient*, would ever presume a local connection here, to Inchkenneth, to people we know day to day. The only thing we don't have is a Sikh in our story – unless you count Tinker Jock as a Sikh! But there we are: Iona, Inchkenneth and the Ross of Mull – they've all been playing their part in the affairs of mankind since the days of Columba. We may be cowherds minding sheep, but we can see as far as the best of sailors and we draw people in, like sirens, to the oldest rocks in the world.

O Iona of my heart, Iona of my love,
Instead of Monks voices shall be the lowing of cattle,
But, before the world come to an end,
Iona shall be as it was.

It's hard to define spiritual values but spiritual values are important for us here just because they exceed the normal limits, the local horizon – things of the spirit remain significant and solid when everything else crumbles, or seems to crumble. I don't think anyone ever put this better than St Paul in Corinthians 13:

Though I speak with the tongues of men and of angels, and have not charity, I am become as sounding brass, or a tinkling cymbal. And though I have the gift of prophecy, and understand all mysteries, and all knowledge; and though I have all faith, so that I can remove mountains, and have not charity, I am nothing. And though I bestow all my goods to feed the poor, and though I give my body to be burned, and have not charity, It profiteth me nothing. Charity suffereth long, and is kind; charity envieth not; charity vaunteth not itslef, is not puffed up, doth not behave itself unseemly, seeketh not her own, is not easily provoked, thinketh no evil; rejoiceth not in iniquity, but rejoiceth in the truth; beareth all things, believeth all things, hopeth all things, endureth all things. Charity never faileth: but whether there be prophecies, they shall fail; whether there be tongues, they shall cease; whether there be knowledge, it shall vanish away.

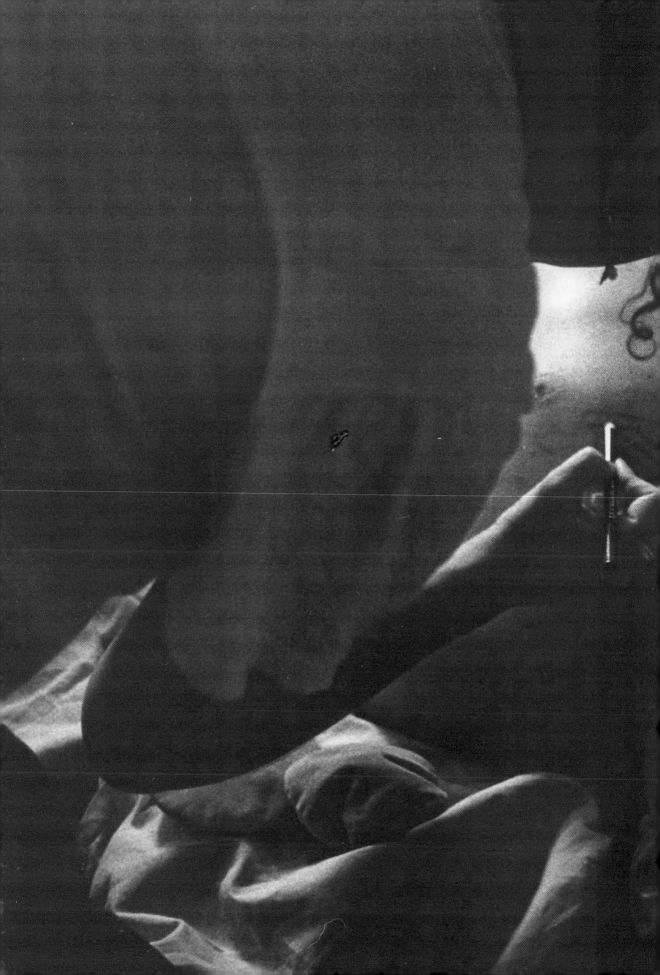

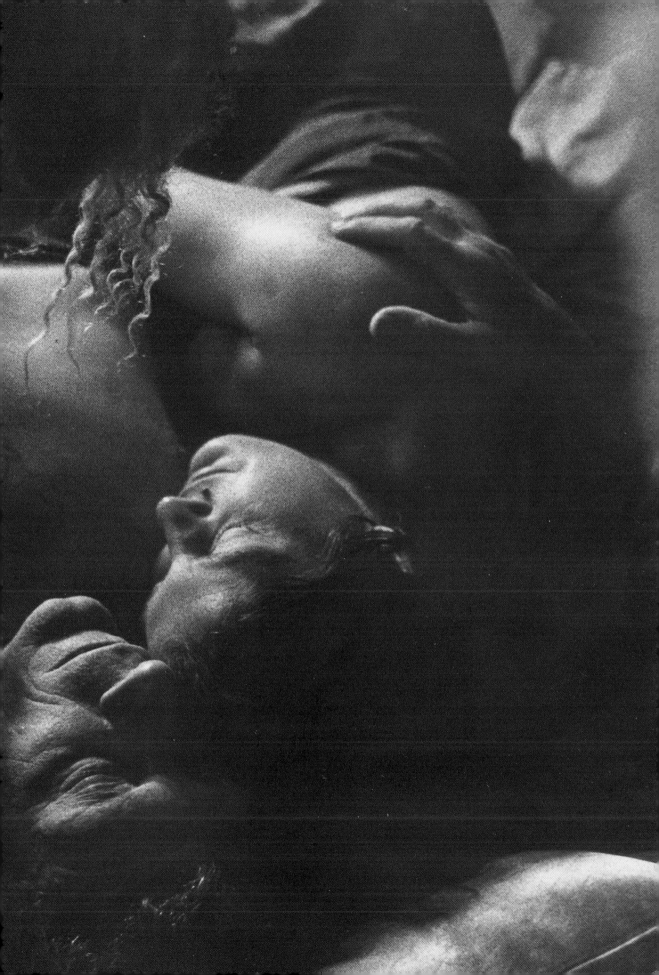

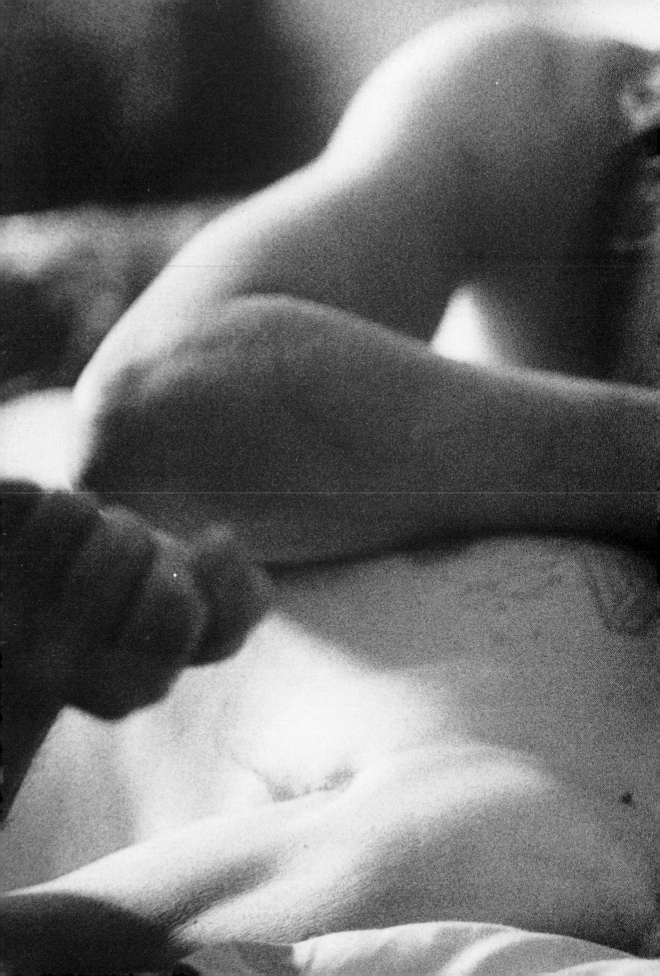

Top.
The German actress,
Angela Winkler, rehearses above
Inchkenneth House, 1992.
(AW)

Bottom.
Angela Winkler as 'Cloud' in
Walk Me Home, *Inchkenneth,*
1992 (AW)

Joujou Ferguson Mitchell

ST KILDA AND PARIS

'Ah! Monsieur l'Eccosais — if only I had met you before I met my husband!'

I was born in Paris on 1st January 1919, but my father, Donald Ferguson, was born in Dumbarton and his father, Neill Ferguson, was born on St Kilda. That was a very long time ago. When he grew up he left the island and went away as an engineer in the navy. He married a woman called Mary Wilkie, the lock-keeper's daughter at Crinan — that's near Lochgilphead in Argyll. She was a Baptist but all the St Kildans were Presbyterians and the Baptist minister told her he could not, he would not, marry her to man from the Church of Scotland! So my grandfather said, 'Don't worry, Mary, my minister will marry us,' and he did. They were very happy and their children were brought up in the Church of Scotland, in Dumbarton.

They had three boys and two girls. The eldest was my uncle, Neill. He went away to Spain as a civil engineer. Then there was my father, Donald Finlay Ferguson, he went to France, as a chartered accountant working for Babcock and Wilcox, the Glasgow engineers. He was born in 1874. Then there was John, he went to Japan and married an English lady. She was dreadful —very grand! Fortunately no offspring ensued. Then there was Tracy, she was very Presbyterian, in the nice sense, and she was very St Kildan looking. She got engaged to a minister who was a missionary. He went away to India but never returned. He was killed, so she never married. So, only one of those five children, Elizabeth, stayed in Scotland. She had two daughters: one died, the other married a man from the island of Mull.

Babcock and Wilcox had a big store at the Coeur Neuf just outside Paris. My father was sent to manage the business and he stayed for forty years. He was a great golfer and there were not many of them in France at that time.

Joujou Ferguson Mitchell collecting
driftwood, Kintyre, 1997. (JFM)

He always played in tweeds made on St Kilda. He was a St Kildan fanatic – he went back almost every year. He was six feet two, walked very straight and always wore his kilt on Sundays. He was a cyclist and a harrier. I remember him running in the long distance race from Paris to Chantilly. He ran with a champagne cork in each hand and a cabbage leaf on his head, to keep off the sun! People were laughing at him – he was over fifty – but he won! Donald Findlay Ferguson. He liked everyone to call him Donald, even his granddaughter. He lived an extraordinary life and I loved him very much.

*Baby Joujou with her mother
and French grandmother,
Paris, 1919.*

He met my mother when she was seven years of age and he fell in love with her and decided to marry her. He decided there on their first meeting, that this wee girl – my mother was always small, just four feet ten inches – would be the woman he would marry. Her name was Marguerite Jeanne Parrot, but everyone called her Mémé. She was the eldest daughter of my father's best friend, Charles Parrot. The two men worked together at Babcock and Wilcox. Donald was very tall, every inch the Highlander. He was always talking about St Kilda. He was aristocratic, handsome, charming, romantic and slightly eccentric.

Joujou with her uncle from
the Auvergne, 1921. (JFM)

My French grandmother adored him! I remember my mother telling me how her
mother would greet Donald saying, 'Ah! Monsieur l'Eccosais – if only I had met
you before I met my husband!'

  When Donald first arrived as a stranger in Paris, the Parrots invited
him out because they thought, 'Oh how lonely Donald must be!' and very soon
he was almost a member of the family. Donald and Charles were the closest of
friends at work and at play. Every Sunday Donald would come for lunch,
beautifully dressed in full Highland regalia. It would be a grand French lunch

which finished with brandy and cigars and all the rest of it. Afterwards Donald would fall asleep in an armchair and the children would be climbing all over him, like Lilliputians on the mountainous Gulliver decked in red tartan and lace! My mother used to draw funny faces on his knees.

Paris before the First World War was a fantastic place and our family had wonderful, happy times. Their life was the life painted by Manet and Monet, Renoir and Degas, Toulouse and Maupaussant. Then, in 1912, at the age of thirty-seven, Charles' young wife Antoinette died and my mother, as the eldest child, was left with her six younger siblings. My mother was, even then, in love with my father and as soon as she reached the age of eighteen, Donald asked Mémé's hand in marriage. That was in 1915. Charles Parrot was not very keen! 'Non, non, non!' I think he thought he was going to lose his best friend! He was worried that their visits to the Café Noir would be finished! Although they had house servants perhaps he thought he was going to lose his best little housekeeper! Anyway, he suddenly came up with all kinds of objections to the marriage. He told my mother, 'You cannot marry Donald, he's a Protestant! He's a foreigner!' All sorts of silly things – to put my mother off!

Well, my mother was still very young and she was always very wee, but she was strong-minded and she had plenty of character and she said, 'Very well Papa! Say what you will, but if you won't let me marry Donald now – I'll wait till I'm twenty-one, and I'll marry Donald then, whether you like it or not!' And that's what she did. It was her uncle who gave her away. They got married in February 1918. My mother was twenty-one and my father was forty-four. In fact they got married four times! At the British Embassy, at the Mairie, in the Eglise Catholique, and at the Scots Kirk in Paris. After all that, my father and grandfather were soon once again the best of friends.

Donald was so proud of the St Kildan people, their survival over thousands of years, their street parliament. He used to go back every summer, right up to the time of the evacuation in 1930. After that, he never went back, and it's a strange thing – he never took my mother and I have never been, nor has my daughter, Martine. I'm now eighty years old and it'll be getting difficult for me to climb the stacks! We have had the opportunity of going, but we've never wanted to go as tourists nor whilst the military was there.

From the time I was a baby, my father used to call me 'the Princess of St Kilda' and tell me wonderful stories of how the women would come down the cliffs laden with puffins and white fulmars and the men would leap down from the boats with sheep on their shoulders. And he would tell stories of the St Kilda wren and the St Kilda mouse! 'One day I'll take you there,' he would say, 'and I will show you the Champs Elysées!' He had written the name up at the bottom of the one street of houses. And who knows if the name is not still there, written in

The St Kilda 'iron' which Donald Ferguson gave his daughter, as a present, on his return to Paris after a summer visit to St Kilda, c.1928. It might be an iron or a hand-quern for grinding oats.
(TN)

his hand? But probably it has long gone with the wind. He was a great romantic.

He always wore a scarf that had been knitted on St Kilda. And my husband always wore a scarf knitted on St Kilda. Donald had suits made of St Kilda tweed. They lasted for years and smelt very strong, especially when it rained. It must have been the urine used in the waulking, and on St Kilda my father said that the smell of the oils from the seabirds pervaded everything on the island. Those suits weren't the best thing to wear on the Metro but they were great when he was biking out in the country. We still have some little faded remnants of St Kildan tweed upstairs. I preserve the relics of St Kilda and the relics of Napoleon. To me, they are like the bones of the saints. And they meant the same to my husband.

Donald used to tell me how he would ask the children on St Kilda, 'What shall I bring you next time I come?' And they used to shout out, 'A tree! A tree!' because there were no trees on the island. And one year he went out for the New Year and he took them a Christmas Tree! Ooooh lala! And on another occasion he took them a bicycle, even though they couldn't ride much on St Kilda. There was no surfaced road. And, of course, every year he brought presents back from St Kilda to Paris. And my mother and her family, in Paris and in the Auvergne, loved the idea of all this: this man who, every year, disappeared out into the Atlantic to visit his relations on an island that wasn't even marked on the map! This island where people had lived on seabirds, driftwood and a few sheep for thousands of years. I still have a little 'flat-iron' made of stone which he brought to Paris and Martine has a driftwood stool from St Kilda. He brought lengths of tweed and knitted garments, birds' eggs and photographs. One of his relations on the mainland had Fergusons, the materials shop in Glasgow, so we were never short of good Scotch cloth.

My father was not only proud of St Kilda, he was proudly Scottish. He always organised a big Hogmanay party every year in Paris and it was in the middle of the celebrations, in 1919, that I was born. With it being the first New Year after the war, it was a great wild party, but Donald, sensible as always, had not forgotten to invite a doctor and midwife! They just moved into the bedroom to deliver me. I was christened Marguarite Antoinette Mary, but when my nanny came in she said, 'Ah, que beau Joujou! What a lovely little toy!' In France presents are given on New Year's Day, so it was Joujou I became and everyone's always called me Joujou to this day.

I was my parents' first and last child. My father said, 'One princess in a family is quite enough!' I was brought up a Catholic, only speaking French. That's what Donald wanted; he was more happy for me to be French. We lived in France, so it was natural that I should be brought up a French-speaking Catholic – like Joan of Arc and Napoleon! They were my great heroes. My one English word was 'daddy'. And my dreams were often about daddy's mist-clad, windswept, magical island – St Kilda. St Kilda embodied all my hopes and desires; it was, to me, everything that St Helena was not. I felt so proud to be attached to St Kilda.

My French ancestors were all country people from the Auvergne and we loved to go down to visit them for holidays, on their beautiful old farms isolated in the mountains. Whenever we were there my father would be saying how beautiful it was, how like Scotland it was. One of my great uncles in the Auvergne had twenty boys, one after the other, then the twenty-first was a girl! So she was called France, and all the children used to call her 'La France'. I remember her very well – she used to ride side-saddle on a donkey and always she was dressed in the traditional Auvergne costume. We would be sitting talking in my grandfather's house when a cry would go up, 'La France arrivée!' and we younger ones would all rush out into the yard and up the track she would be coming, very slowly, on her donkey, as if she were in a painting by Corot. She looked very old to me then, but I think she would only have been forty or fifty, certainly not as old as the République! 'La France! La France! La France arrivée!' They were survivors too, in the Auvergne! It's a very mountainous area and the roads in those days were very poor. The place was not isolated like St Kilda, but it was as far from what people call 'civilisation' as the deep glens of the north-west Highlands. Auvergne is 'La France Profond' – they call it that. It's beautiful; up near Salaire it's very beautiful.

In the 'twenties the old patois language of Auvergne was still very much alive and it was the people like our people who kept it going. Now it's coming back into fashion, like Gaelic.

My nanny was from the Auvergne. I called her 'Zizi' – her name was Louise, but Zizi was easy, much easier for a child I liked her, and coming from

Joujou Ferguson with Zizi, her nanny
from the Auvergne, 1919 (JFM)

the Auvergne, she naturally spoke the patois and it became almost natural to me. We used to visit her old maman. She lived in a beautiful old stone cottage, and I remember her saying – thinking I wouldn't understand – 'Louise, she's bored, can't you find her a doll to play with?' The old lady thought I wouldn't understand, but I did and Zizi replied, 'Don't worry, I'm going to make one!' And she took a poker and put it in the fire and she got a log and burned eyes and nose and mouth into the wood and made two stick arms and clothed the doll with some old rags her mother found – and it was a most wonderful doll. Oh I loved that doll and I took it back to Paris and put it in the middle of all my grand French dolls – and that was my favourite.

One of my Auvergne grand-uncles lived to be 101! Good food, good water, good wine, good exercise and a healthy shortage of *l'petit bourgeoisie!* They were in short supply in the Auvergne – those half-baked respectable people with their interest in money and small talk and what people think about the behaviour of neighbours! *Les peasants de L'Auvergne.* They worked and they lived their lives – and so many of them were killed in the war. The children of those twenty sons were cannon-fodder at Verdun.

Going down to the south we were great admirers of the Cathars and the Knights Templar and the old traditions of the free-thinkers. All our family were free-thinkers and radicals. When the Templars were suppressed in France many of them came into Scotland and many are buried here in Argyll. *Liberté, Equalité, Fraternité* – both Donald and my husband loved those ideals and lived and worked for them. And those ideals gave joy.

My father knew the whole of France. He would disappear on his bicycle; he explored the whole country. Once he was there in the Jura, when a very heavy thunderstorm came on. He was miles out in the country – the landscape of Courbet – night was falling and he didn't know where to go. Through the down-pouring rain he made for a large building and knocked on the door. It was a monastery. Of course he was asked to come in, and he very quickly became a friend of the abbot, who insisted my father come again whenever he liked. And after that Donald would suddenly take his bike and disappear into La Jura for weeks at a time. The monks were very good to him. They took him into the secret parts of their library and let him read and look at the most beautiful painted manuscripts, never shown to the public. He used to just say 'Jeu mon vie,' and we knew daddy was off to the Jura.

Donald always went alone to the monastery, just as he always went alone to St Kilda. There was something monastic about his character. He had the austere, spartan energy of the old Celtic saints, but he also boldly enjoyed all the good things of life, especially the cuisine and comforts my mother provided. He had a slightly wicked sense of humour and, coming back from La Jura, he used to compliment the food served in the abbey, how simple it was, all home-grown and home-made and perfect. That used to annoy my mother, just a little! She was a great cook – very rich, very French. Great times we had at the table, laughing and laughing.

Donald Findlay Ferguson was a very good singer and he liked to sing the songs of Robert Burns. 'A Man's a Man for a' that', 'My Love is Like a Red, Red Rose' and many others. Like Burns, Donald was a natural humanitarian and he imbued me and all those around him with his values. Race, colour, creed – everyone was to be respected and treated well. I was proud to follow his example. Once a new teacher came to our school in Paris. And on the first day she told us 'I am Protestant from Nîmes, but, of course, I shall not allow that to influence my teaching.' At playtime we were all talking about this and about how her ancestors might have been killed by our ancestors in the St Bartholomew Day Massacres. We became very upset and made a collection for her and I went to my mother's florist and we bought flowers. And the florist gave us an especially big and beautiful bouquet because my parents were good clients of that shop. We took the flowers to the Protestant teacher, and she asked, 'Why are you giving

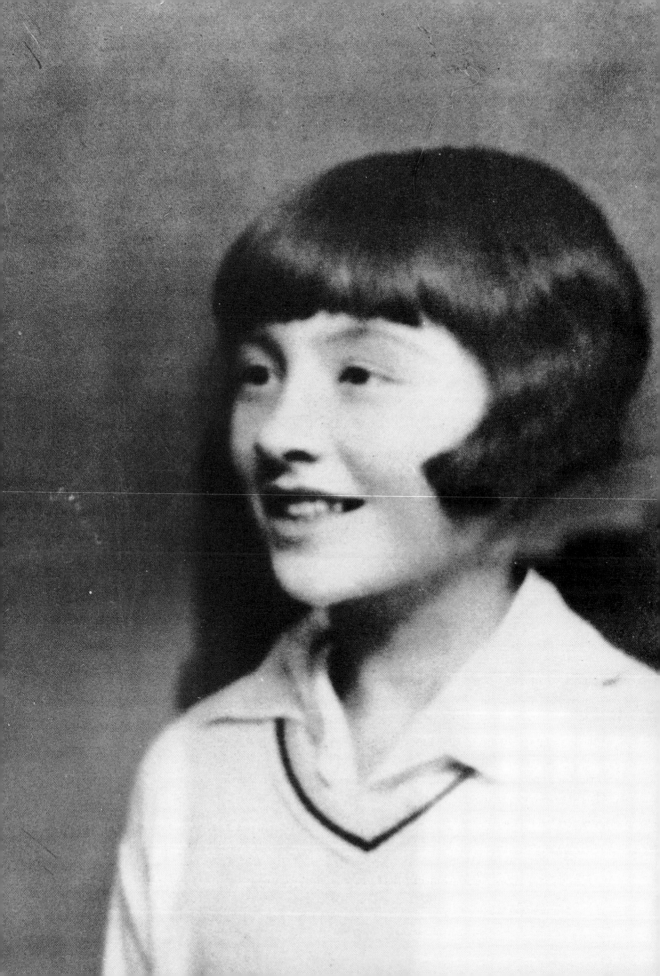

me these beautiful flowers?' and we said 'It's because we're so sorry we killed your ancestors,' and she started to cry and she said, 'I wish the whole world was like you. You don't know what you have done.'

There is a saying, 'France has never recovered from the Dreyfus affair!' My French grandfather was a Dreyfusar, and my father and my husband of course were strong supporters of Dreyfus. It was much talked about in Paris when I was a girl. There was a boycott of French goods in Great Britain and my father said it was a big issue in Scotland. But here, of course, it was soon forgotten, whereas in France the arguments went on and on. We had many Jewish friends and various children came to my school as refugees. One was a beautiful boy who was a brilliant pianist. One was a girl with whom I became very friendly and I asked her to come home with me. She said, 'Yes, I would like to, but first you must tell your parents I'm Jewish.' When I did that my father was so angry he shouted. That any schoolgirl should have felt she had to say that in France was an unpardonable disgrace.

I remember an older girl called Jacqueline Bloch, whose mother died. I knew this and when I saw her on the stairs I was surprised to see she was dressed in red. In France, even the children dressed in black after a death in the family, so I said, 'Jacqueline, your mother is dead and you are dressed in red?' She replied, 'That I am dressed in red does not mean I am not broken-hearted. It is in your heart that you wear mourning.' That too was a lesson to me. Another of my good friends, Florette, died in Auschwitz. One of my Catholic aunties was in a camp. She was arrested by the Germans, in Nancy, for distributing leaflets and being out after the curfew. She told us later she was so cold in that camp she decided that if she ever got out she'd live somewhere warm. We're a funny family. In the 'sixties she married a Moroccan, a Muslim, twenty years younger than she was. Now she's eighty-eight and he's been dead these many years, but she's still out there in Agadir enjoying the sun and the sea, reading her books and sweeping men off their feet.

My father would always like to support the oppressed, the underdog. In the First World War he continued to work for Babcocks in Paris, but he also did a great deal of work for the wellbeing of the poor. He took adult education evening classes; he arranged the installation of showers and improved the housing conditions of working men and their families. One day, I was looking for a pencil when I found a little purple button-hole. It was the 'Officiel de la Academie Balzac'! When I asked my father why he did not wear it, he said 'My dear daughter, a Scotsman has no need to wear a little bit of coloured ribbon!' He was flamboyant but against show.

I remember the day a telegram came from Scotland saying my grandmother was ill. My mother said, 'Donald you must go at once!'

'Why?' said Donald. 'Because your mother may be dying!' said

Opposite.
Joujou Ferguson at school in Paris, c.1930 (JFM)

maman. 'Perhaps not!' said my father. But my mother persuaded him to go back to Scotland and soon we had another telegram, 'Mother has died, must stay one week. Donald.' A week passed and I went with my mother, three of my aunties and my godfather to meet him, on his return, at the Gare du Nord. My mother was all in black and behind her my aunties were all dressed in deep mourning. My godfather was in black and I, who was just eight years of age, had black shoes and black socks and a dark purple coat. I remember it so well – there we were in the steam and smoke of the great station and my father was coming towards us. Suddenly he stopped, and he went white in the face, then he rushed towards us saying, 'Oh Jean, que bien? Votre mère?' And she replied, 'Non, non, Donald! Votre mère!' He had not thought for a moment that we, in Paris, would be mourning *his* mother! That broke the ice! And when we got home, he unpacked a beautiful kilt he had bought me from Forsyths in Glasgow, in the Ferguson tartan, and he asked me to put it on. Maman said, 'Non Donald, she cannot wear it!'

'Why not?' said my father. 'There is red in the tartan!' said my mother! 'But this is our clan!' said my father. They almost had an argument! The compromise was that I wore my kilt, with a white shirt and a wee black ribbon – pour ma grandmère d'Ecosse.

Joujou with friend, Paris, summer 1933. (JFM)

We came to Scotland in 1938, partly because my father was due to retire, but more because he knew another war with Germany was coming. It was a big shock for my mother and I to come from Paris to Glasgow in 1938. I had never been to Scotland. But I had heard so much from my father and read so much about Mary, Queen of Scots and Ivanhoe – and I thought Glasgow would be like Paris on the banks of Loch Lomond! And Glasgow was full of broken bottles and children with no shoes or socks on. It was dreadful – Mon Dieu! My mother could speak hardly a word of English, but we had a nice house and very soon I married my beloved husband, Edward Roslyn Mitchell.

Eddie had been born in England, in Wiltshire, but that was a mistake – his father was a travelling lay preacher from near Huntly in Aberdeenshire who just happened to be in Wiltshire when the time came. His mother was a Yorkshire woman. They had a large family and soon settled in Glasgow. Eddie went to Glasgow University and became a lawyer in Glasgow. When I met him, he was a widower. When he saw me he stopped and said, 'You are from St Kilda! I can tell by your high cheeks and the colours in your hair!' Well we just clicked and that was that. He was almost fifty-nine, and I was just nineteen. He had two grown-up children, Nora and Ian. They were older than I! And later on, Ian used to take great pleasure in introducing me as 'ma maman', a woman much younger than himself! It's the kind of thing they'd present on Channel 4 today, not as a joke but as something salacious. Eddie was a Quaker. He loved St Kilda, he loved France. He had been a Glasgow City councillor and

Above left.
Joujou Ferguson Mitchell, as she
was during the war years in Glasgow
working for the Free French.
(JFM)

Above right.
Eddie Roslyn Mitchell, Glasgow
city councillor, MP and lawyer, as
he was a few years before he met and
married Joujou Ferguson in
1939. (JFM)

Labour MP for Paisley. Like me he had a great admiration for Napoleon and the Revolutionary Republic.

I remember going to a talk, at the university, by the Marquis of Bute, about St Kilda. I was with both my father and my husband and afterwards we talked with the marquis. When he was introduced to me, he looked at me sternly – then he took out his gold watch on its chain. He said, 'Look, Joujou's teeth!' He'd once visited our house in Paris, when I was just a wee girl, and he'd given me his watch to play with and I'd tested it with my teeth! He said to my husband, 'These·are the teethmarks of your wife!' And it was true, there was a half-moon of teethmarks on each side of his watch! Later his daughter and her husband had come for there honeymoon to Paris, and they'd visited us and we'd entertained them. And the marquis said that on their return to Scotland, his daughter told him, 'I've never seen anything so beautiful as the Tour Eiffel – or the salon de Madame Ferguson!'

Edward Roslyn Mitchell first became a Glasgow councillor in 1909, ten years before I was born. He joined the Labour Party and he did a great

Joujou Mitchell on the 'plane steps and Eddie Mitchell in kilt prepare to fly to France to give support to the city of Brest, 1945. (JFM)

deal for the establishment of Catholic state education in Glasgow. He became a close friend of Hugh Robertson of the Orpheus Choir in Glasgow and he sang in the choir. He was also interested in the druids and was very pleased to know that I used to go out cutting the mistletoe at Christmas and New Year. But he was disappointed that my cutting was done not with a golden sickle but Zizi's cut-throat razor! He had been out to the Hebrides and St Kilda collecting folksongs; he was a friend of Margerie Kennedy Fraser. Once he got to know St Kilda, he became fascinated by the St Kildan people and their history. He and my father got on very well. He had a great collection of photographs of the island.

Eddie was a Quaker, but he was a rational humanist and an agnostic rather than a believer. He believed that Jesus Christ was the most marvellous man that ever lived, the model for all men, but he found it difficult to believe in the unique divinity of Christ, which is something also true of the Jews. The druids didn't present that kind of metaphysical problem! They were just human beings with powers and skills. He wrote poems, songs and stories; he wrote for the

Joujou and Eddie on holiday in the Highlands, 1950s. (JFM)

Glasgow Herald. He enjoyed life, very much as my father did. Sometimes when my daughter, Martine, got older she would get annoyed with us, in the mornings, because we laughed so much! She thought it was obscene. We used to have breakfast in bed. I would go downstairs, make breakfast for everyone and take it up to them in bed – to Martine, my mother, any visitors we might have, and to my husband. Then we would take our time and enjoy ourselves. Martine would say, 'Why should your breakfast last two hours! And why do you laugh all the time!' Two things I have always especially enjoyed doing, lighting the fire and making the breakfast. I always did that in the Girl Guides. It must be my Palaeolithic ancestry imposing itself!

Eddie and Joujou with daughter, Martine, 1950s (JFM)

Like Donald, Eddie was a great lover of Burns. In 1930 he gave the Immortal Memory from the farmhouse of Mossgiel, where Burns wrote many of his greatest poems. It was a great anniversary gathering and the whole evening was broadcast on the BBC – not just to Britain, but to the Dominions, to America and the whole world. He began, 'If these walls could speak, how gladly would we be silent. If they could take tongue and say: "One day, I mind how he came in from the harrowing. His eyes were glowing, but he seemed to see nothing …" why, the whole world would be waiting for us to report what they heard …' And he went on, 'The poet was here for two years – two years – yet the world would never be the same, for him or for us …' Eddie was a wonderful speaker and conversationalist. He defeated Mr Asquith at the Paisley by-election in 1924 by over 7000 votes and it was said that was due to his moral vision, his genuine social concern and his ability to speak on the platforms. He excited great enthusiasm in his audiences. I have a press cutting from the *Border Telegraph* of March 30th 1926. That was the year of the National Strike and this is what the paper said:

In the fight for emancipation that will strike the fetters of private monopoly off the limbs of democracy and give the people economic liberation, few men in the future will play a larger part in that liberation than Mr Roslyn Mitchell. He will do much to supply the moral fervour and the large purpose. He does not track and trim, but keeps to the well charted highway and the open sea. It is breadth of appeal that has made him one of the powerful orators in the English-speaking world. His appeal is always to the moral conscience. The name of the Almighty is as familiar on his lips as the name of Gladstone. It is the highest tribute to Mr Mitchell's sincerity that employing it he never gives a sense of canting. The truth is that he lives in an atmosphere out of which our politics has largely passed. Few men today, in the House of Commons, ever touch the spiritual note. The oratory that fell to earth when Gladstone and Bright ceased to wing it with spiritual passion has again been expounded with great sincerity by Mr Mitchell, who perceives that religion is a concern that has to do with the family, the city, and the nation, with business and with politics, as well as what is called the individual life. All his political thinking springs out this soil of moral ideas. In such a case a century may elapse between the sowing of the wind and the reaping of the whirlwind, but the one follows the other. Mr Roslyn Mitchell's heart beats true to his first and only love – the working people. He can chastise them, but he loves them, not with the aloofness of a superior person but with the love of a comrade, who offers them a shining example …

Eddie Roslyn Mitchell had a love for all people of all races. He was very moved when, in a group conversation, one of his friends replied to the question, 'What do you consider the greatest moment in history?' with this unequivocal answer, 'The carrying of the body of David Livingston by African natives from Chitambo's village to Zanzibar … That was the greatest example in history of a sudden leap in evolution. The men who did that miracle leaped 5000 years from savagery into a higher ethical realm than we have yet reached. They apprehended a something outwith their powers of reason, that led them without thought of reward to do this deed. No one can tell why they did it. They were impelled by some power which took possession of them. It was not superstition, for in their journey they broke through a thousand age-long superstitions. What it was I cannot tell, but it was the greatest event and the greatest romance in human history.' That man who spoke knew one of the natives who had carried Livingstone. His name was Matthew Wellington, and at that moment he was still alive, eighty-five years of age, and living in Mombasa.

One of my favourite pieces of Eddie's journalism was titled 'The Two Crusaders'. It tells you such a lot about what he loved and believed important.

Joujou and Martine, early 1950s. (JFM)

It stands in a little walled graveyard in the Isle of Islay, beside the Golden Sands where the road branches off to the Mull of Oa. It is a plain cross of wood, black with creosote that it may last a few extra years. In white is recorded the title, 'A Negro unidentified'.

On 6th February, 1918, the liner *Tuscania*, bearing soldiers of the United States to Europe, was sunk by a German submarine near the rugged rocks of the Oa. In time the bodies of the men were washed ashore in the bay and were laid to rest in this little graveyard, specially prepared for them. And there they lay in peace, British sailors, American soldiers and the 'Negro unidentified'.

In time the citizens of the United States sent over a commission to the graveyard by the sea to bring back to America the bodies of their young citizens. Reverently the young soldiers were removed. The 'Negro unidentified' was left.

At the Point of the Oa the women of the United States reared a great tower, from which the American Eagle spreads his mighty wings, in honour of the white Crusaders. But the unknown warrior, whose ancestors British slave-dealers shipped to America, still lies beside the sea – but not alone. In the ancient churchyard fifty yards away there lies another unknown warrior. His grave is marked by a large slab of stone on which is carved the figure of a Crusader of the olden time, in full armour. None can tell who he was, save that he was an ancient chief who went forth from the Isle to the Holy Land and came back to the little green place beside the Golden Sands. Centuries of time span those fifty yards between the unknown crusader and the 'Negro unidentified'.

If I were a citizen of the United States, I would go back and tell the people of the companionship of those two Crusaders. And I should ask my friends to join with me in setting up over the grave of the 'Negro unidentified' a statue in black marble of a Negro looking from the Isle of the Hebrides over the sea that leads to Africa and America. It would then be that, just as all who see the Crusader in the old kirkyard link up the centuries as they look upon his figure, so would all who see the Negro link up three races and three continents in the figure of the unknown African Negro who came from America for the salvation of Europe.

Joujou Ferguson Mitchell at home, Kintyre, 1999.

And through the Second World War, Eddie and I and my mother all worked hard for Free French forces in Glasgow – to free Europe for a second time. Donald was by then quite an old man. Although he liked Glasgow and felt at home, he really missed France and the life of Paris. And my mother always found English difficult and she never really understood Glasgow. During the war she would walk into pubs as though they were cafés! And drink whisky as though it were wine! But she was such a strong character that she never had any trouble from anyone! The great centres of her life were Donald first, Paris second, the Auvergne third and Glasgow fourth. When my father died, in 1952, Mémé came to live with Eddie and me but though she was only fifty-three at the time, she seemed to give up. She still had me and Martine, but she died in 1962. For three generations our husbands have died whilst we women were young. My mother was fifty-three when Donald died, I was forty-six when Eddie died, and Martine was fifty-two when her husband Bernard Chalmers died.

But we have always been optimistic people – the Fergusons – and the Mitchells and the Chalmers. The St Kildans had to be! I remember the painter J. D. Fergusson and Margaret Morris, the great Celtic dancer, visiting us in Paris (we were the only two Fergusons in the telephone directory). They too were wonderful optimists. Ferguson's nude paintings are full of brimming life. He loved sunshine and flowers; his work is full of 'the mirth of the sunblest south'! When they too came back to Glasgow they often used to visit us in Bearsden.

If you survived life on St Kilda you had to be tough and never be down. Life was hard but timeless and unchanging and this bred a confidence and a strange joyful stoicism in the people. We're still a family of optimists. Perhaps that's also because we believe in God, on both sides of the family – we always have. The life of the St Kildans was founded on a rock! And the Auvergne has been inhabited by the same people for 30,000 years. People of the sea and people of the mountains. Some of the St Kildans had dark eyes but my father had those blue, far-away eyes, eyes that can see for miles; eyes used to an empty horizon; eyes coloured by the sea. My grandson, Damien, has them yet and the long St Kildan toes. His second toe is much longer than his big toe! And mine are just the same. No shoes have ever fitted me! I have bunions like the mountains of the moon!

I told you about my little stone 'iron' from St Kilda. It fits the hand so nicely and it was used to iron the frills the island women wore on their bonnets. It's just a natural stone that suits a particular purpose, but it looks like a Henry Moore sculpture. Recently someone told me they thought the stone was more likely to be a grain grinder than an iron, but it was as an 'iron' my father gave it to me and that's what I'll always keep it as. Of course, the St Kildans did grind all their own corn. It was thrashed and put in a tub made of straw, like an inverted beehive, then hot stones were thrown in to scorch and toast the grain. Then it was ground down in handmills by the women, sitting on the ground. After that, the rough flour was sieved through a sheepskin, stretched on a hoop perforated with holes burnt by a hot wire. During the winter evenings, my father said you would hear women grinding away in almost every house in the village.

The St Kildans were great talkers, loud talkers, and talking seems to run like a genetic force in our family. My daughter, Martine, is a great talker. Donald was, and my grandfather was. Since I was a girl, people have told me I talk too much, and too loud! I've never been afraid to say what I've wanted to people directly. We are what we are. I think that after the famous Martin Martin, the best writer on St Kilda was Sands. He described the voices of the St Kildans as loud and bawling and, he said, very often they spoke all at once! Oh dear, oh dear, whatever next! I don't know whether those voices were developed to deal with the roar of the sea and the constant wind, or whether they were just an expression of the people's enthusiastic and over-generous natures. So poor, and yet so generous and kind. Small things would mean so much for them. A tree! 'Seol! Seol! – A sail! A sail!' Can you imagine that being shouted and everybody running to the shore! Even the minister might get excited at that – for in the old days the boat would call only once a year. We were more cut off on St Kilda than they were on Tristan da Cunha. 'Seol! Seol!' That was something worth shouting about.

Opposite top.
Hirte, nesting place of the solan goose. (ERM)

Opposite bottom.
Bay of Hirte and Dune Island, sheep fanks in foreground. (ERM)

Overleaf.
St Kilda, in the village. (ERM)

Previous page, left.
St Kilda. Collecting gannets. (ERM)

Previous page, right.
St Kilda. Collecting the fulmars.
(ERM)

This page and opposite.
St Kilda. Leaving the island home.
A last look. (ERM)

Above.
St Kilda Post Office. (ERM)

Below.
St Kilda. Eddie Mitchell,
Mrs Ferguson and Mr J.A. (ERM)

Left.
St Kilda. The children. (ERM)

Below.
St Kilda. The Street. (ERM)

Above.
St Kilda. Aunt Gillies, née Ferguson,
overcome with shyness.

Below.
St Kilda. The Street.

Opposite.
Finlay MacQueen, last President
of the St Kilda Parliament
aboard the evacuation ship.

Overleaf.
A ceilidh on the
Dunara at Scalpay.

My daughter, Martine, was a teacher and headmistress, so her St Kildan voice was perfect in the classroom, with rain and wind rattling the windows. She's a romantic like me; very French, very Scots, very St Kildan. She's got a story just as strange as mine. So I'll let her speak – for a moment!

MARTINE MITCHELL

I never knew my great-grandfather, Neill Ferguson, but I loved my grandfather very much. He always insisted I called him Donald. He refused to be called anything but Donald. Maybe it went back to the sense of equality of the St Kildans – young and old, everyone equal. He used to take me on the most amazing walks, long walks out of Glasgow to where the badger sets were. He loved nature; he was always looking out for eagles. He still ran as a harrier in his old age. Nobody could ask for a kinder grandfather than Donald Ferguson. I really loved him. I was twelve when he died. That was in 1952; he was seventy-nine. He's buried in Dumbarton, beside his father, Neill. Neither has a headstone. Donald said he didn't want a headstone until one was brought from St Kilda. He said no other stone should lie on his breast.

Opposite.
Martine Mitchell, daughter of
Joujou Ferguson and Eddie Mitchell,
c.1964.

I've got my mother's red hair but its my son Damien who has inherited that very long second toe that seems to have evolved amongst the St Kildans, because of their centuries as barefooted rock climbers. Joujou has them, and it's made her life very difficult! No shoes fit her – she has terrible bunions. We all have narrow feet with long, long toes, like the feet of Jesus in the early crucifixion paintings. Maybe it was his descendants went out to St Kilda! Damien's second toe is so long it curls right over his big toe. Prehensile, like a monkey's! He's six feet tall but like a wire. He's got long arms and strong fingers; he'd make an excellent rock-climber, or a plumber! My daughter, Damaris, is a music student. She's inherited the musical talent of the Fergusons. They are both away studying; Damaris in Edinburgh, Damien in Dundee.

I was born in Glasgow but Joujou brought me up as a native French speaker. I went to Westbourne School for Girls. It's now part of Glasgow Academy. I studied history and French, then went to Notre Dame Teacher Training College. I became a teacher. Then I went into educational television and I got a job presenting for the BBC. But teaching was always my first love and I gave up television and came out to Kintyre, to the Atlantic coast, to be headmistress of Rhunahaorine Primary School, here at Tayinloan. It was a wild place in the days before I came, tinkers in one classroom, all the rest in another! A special van ferried the tinkers; a small coach took the others! I knew something about discrimination myself. Going for a job in Glasgow, I remember one

Opposite.
Martine on holiday in France.
(MMC)

Above.
Martine Mitchell photographed at
the Consular Ball, Glasgow, 1958.
This is the photograph that attracted
the attention of the curate, Bernard
Chalmers. (MMC)

Below.
Martine Mitchell as a young
reporter working for the BBC,
c.1963. (MMC)

Bernard Chalmers. (MMC)

interviewer asking what school I had gone to. When I said Westbourne School for Girls, he smiled and said, 'Oh that's fine. We don't want Catholics here!' I said, 'But I am a Catholic!' And that was the end of it! My father felt very strongly about those kinds things. It was he who was primarily responsible for the Education Act of 1918 which allowed Catholics to have state schooling in Scotland. E. Roslyn Mitchell. Politics was his life and it was an extremely busy and wide-ranging life. And Joujou was also active. She became president of the Français d'Ecosse. She worked with De Gaulle and the Free French through the war. She and Eddie organised Glasgow's campaign to rebuild the port Brest in Brittany. Every Christmas she still hosts a special Christmas party for all the French children in Glasgow.

I taught here at Rhumahaorine for twenty years, then, after my husband died, I took early retirement. Now both Joujou and I spend a lot of time in the Auvergne, but strangely, neither of us has ever been out to St Kilda. We're

still hoping to go. One of my former pupils here, Clare Toms, has married one of the Search and Rescue helicopter pilots for the Western Isles, so we're hoping he'll take us out to St Kilda – take us home! Out into the Atlantic. We're a strange family, no doubt, but we like ourselves and we enjoy ourselves.

      I liked working in broadcasting but I didn't enjoy the back-biting. During the final weeks of my employment at the Beeb, I really enjoyed myself! One evening I went over to the BBC Club celebrating with friends. We had a great night, then I had to go back to read the late news and the fishing forecast. It seems to have been the most outstanding fishing forecast ever put out over the airwaves! Very memorable it still is amongst the fishermen. The Herring! The Minches! Rock Salmon off Rockall! The Herring! When I came here to be interviewed for the post of headmistress, the local procurator fiscal met me with open arms, saying 'Aaaah Martine – THE HERRING!' It was an amazing fishing forecast! I've heard that the fishermen are talking about it yet. I read it with great

Martine Mitchell and Bernard Chalmers, newly wed, Kintrye, 1978. (MMC)

feeling! I cast my bread upon the waters. And I don't regret it. That was my swansong at the BBC. It's gone into folklore!

The story of my marriage is almost as interesting as Joujou's. In December 1959, I went to the consular ball in Glasgow and the next day my picture appeared as the 'bouquet girl' in the *Scottish Daily Express*. And it happened that a man called Bernard Chalmers saw this photograph in the paper and he liked it. He showed it to one of his colleagues. 'Well, John,' he said, 'if I was ever to get married, that's the woman I should marry!' He was a curate at Glasgow Cathedral. A priest. He cut the picture out and kept it in his wallet, and he showed it to nobody for eighteen years, till he showed it to me – on our wedding day. And even then he put it straight back in his wallet for safe-keeping. His name was Bernard Mary Chalmers.

Six weeks after the consular ball, on 22nd January 1960, Bernard and I met for the first time. I was nineteen and he was twenty-eight. We gradually became good friends. Over the next eighteen years, never a week went by when we didn't see each other, speak to each other, phone or write to each other and we married on 22nd July 1978, after Bernard had become layisised and given special dispensation by the Pope to marry. One of the telegrams read at our wedding was, 'Patience is a Virtue!' It was a lovely wedding, particularly because so many of Bernard's clergy friends and religious colleagues were there and they were so kind and generous to us.

Bernard was born in Kent but brought up in Scotland. His grandfather was an Aberdeenshire man and his mother was an Edinburgh woman whose mother had come from County Cork in Ireland. That's why his family was Catholic – Chalmers being a very Protestant name. Chalmers was one of the great Presbyterian divines. They were a deeply spiritual family, as were the Fergusons, but there are also secular connections between the Fergusons and the Chalmers; both families designed and built tractors! And, by some strange coincidence, in the graveyard at Dumbarton, where Donald and Neill Ferguson lie buried, the stone next to their graves is dedicated to a Chalmers – a man we don't yet know.

Joujou and I have been friends all my life. She and father had a beautiful relationship. Though there was nearly forty years age-difference between them, rarely have I seen two people so happy together. My father would like to introduce Joujou to people saying, 'France has given me its greatest decoration and honour. This is my wife, Joujou …' And at home, every afternoon, Joujou would be keeping half an eye on the clock and when it got close to five she would be off to the bedroom and make herself beautiful to receive her husband. And always she would be there to welcome him through the door. Every day without fail. It was like Romeo and Juliet, not for one night but ten thousand. They enjoyed life so much, they shared so many interests, and they were so perceptive. I remember my mother telling me how my father noticed Bernard looking at me at a Vocations Exhibition at the Kelvin Hall in May 1960. He leaned across and said, 'My darling, that boy is in love with our daughter!' She said, 'Don't be silly Eddie, he's a priest!' And he said, 'Joujou, I know. And the Church is very cruel!' And things were hard for Bernard and I but slowly, over the years, things shaped themselves, as they had for Donald and my grandmother, and we were often very happy. At last, we were married. We have two beautiful children. And in the end it was not the Church that was cruel but circumstance and fate. We were on holiday in the Auvergne when Bernard died. He had a terrible fall going down steps into the cellar. He was fifty-four.

Both my father and grandfather talked a lot about the St Kilda they knew but my knowledge of the island has also had to rely on books – fortunately there is no shortage of books on St Kilda. I think Eddie's photographs are some of the best photos ever taken on the island and like Joujou I think the best old book is *Out of the World,* or *Life in St Kilda* by J. Sand. It was published in 1877. It was the product of two visits to the island, one of seven weeks in 1875 and one of eight months in 1876–77. Sand was there just a few years after my great grandfather left the island to work at sea. Sand was very factual, for example, he lists all the products exported from St Kilda in 1875.

Cloth	– 227 yds of 47 inches and thumb at	2s 3d
Blankets	– 403 yds of 47 inches and thumb at	1s 10d
Fulmar oil	– 906 pints (equal to 5 pints Imperial)	1s 0d
Tallow	– 17 stones 6lbs (1 stone = 24lbs)	6s 6d
Black feathers	– 86 stones 15lbs	6s 0d
Grey feathers	– 69 stones 19lbs	5s 0d
Cheese	– 38 stones 6lbs	6s 0d
Fish	– 1080 salted ling etc.	each 0s 7d

That year the islanders also sent away twenty first-year stirks and other cattle described as 'being the property of Neill Ferguson, ground officer'. That might have been my great-grandfather, or it might have been one of his relations – I don't know. There is not much solid information about the genealogy of the St Kildans but Sand states that the islanders believed their ancestors came from Uist. They certainly didn't like the people of Harris, their nearest neighbours. That's where the smallpox that devastated the population in 1730 came from. The six family names on St Kilda were – MacQueen, Gillies, Ferguson, MacDonald, MacKinnon and MacCrimmon.

There were three chapels on St Kilda – dedicated to Christ, St

Bernard and Martine Chalmers with their children, Damien and Damaris, 1989. (MMC)

Columba and St Brendan. The culture was Celtic with Norwegian influences but most of the population was almost certainly pre-Celtic. Some were dark, some were fair, they were not generally tall but had long arms, fingers and toes. Only two of the islanders were bald – most had strong thick hair, as I have and as Joujou has. Martin Martin, the first man to describe life on St Kilda at the end of the seventeenth century stated that 'their habit antieently was of sheep-skins'. And, when I was a girl, having heard so many stories from Joujou and Eddie, I used to imagine the giant Polymephus living in a cave on St Kilda, and Odysseus landing in the bay, and the sound of his boat awaking the giant and his great head, with one eye, rising from amongst the sheep gathered in his cave …

The St Kildan sheep were dark woolled and not sheered but plucked by hand. They were far too small and skinny to be worth exporting as meat. They were bred for their wool and only occasionally eaten. Food on the island was nutritious – if you liked oily bird flesh. The economy was a solid subsistence economy, but also precarious. Sand was witness to semi-starvation and my father and all the Fergusons were always indignant and angry at the manner in which the MacLeods of Dunvegan, who owned the island, continued to exploit St Kilda and the St Kildan people into modern times. For them Hirta was a feudal fiefdom. Sand was also appalled by the depressive dictatorial control exercised over the islanders by the Free Church Minister, Mr MacKay. He was very egocentric, puritannical and very hard, but he was genuinely religious. The island, with its parliamentary tradition, seems to have been free of bigotry, thieving and murder. But there are records of one lunatic who became a religious fanatic, Ruari Mhor. He lived in Martin Martin's time. He pretended, or believed, he was John the Baptist and is said to have terrorised the men and debauched 'the weaker' women. He seems to have been the only St Kildan who ever wilfully abused his fellow islanders and even he, finally, saw the light and confessed his sins before the Presbytery on Skye. But, and this is amazing, parts of his ranting sermons lived on in island folklore for 200 years! Sand heard an islander called Og reciting Ruari Mhor's sermons as entertainment for the islanders in the 1870s. Thus, although the St Kildans had been totally cowed by Mr MacKay, they had turned Ruari Mhor into slapstick comedy! But that story also shows how limited the sources of public entertainment on St Kilda were.

Sand was ashamed of the lack of responsibility assumed by the British Government towards St Kilda and its citizens. He believed 'the Empire' had a duty towards St Kilda – but it never fulfilled it and the islanders were left to sink or swim. Sand himself raised the money for a new sea-going boat to give the St Kildans some independence from their master on Skye. It was a splendid new boat made at Ardrisaig and it was towed out on his second visit. The boat was received with great rejoicing but it made no long term difference, partly because Mr MacKay persuaded the islanders not to risk any kind of action independent of MacLeod of Dunvegan.

The people of St Kilda were non-violent and naturally trusting. Unfortunately, outsiders were not usually worth their trust. The islanders' one 'normal' suspicion was of the Harris men. 'Se aite bochd – mosach – salach a-tha ann' were the words used to describe Harris – meaning that it was an inhospitable place of mean and dirty people, and it is not surprising that after the evacuation the St Kildans settled not in the Outer Hebrides, but around Fort William and in Argyll. The St Kildans were bright and adaptive, but their life on the island was so unusual that everywhere else must have seemed very strange to them. Glasgow, in all its Victorian Grandeur, and squalor, must have come like something out of the book of Revelations!

Even the island of Lewis could spring surreal surprises. Whilst waiting to embark on his voyage to St Kilda, Sand describes a visit he made from Stornaway to a graveyard on the island of St Colme:

Bernard Chalmers (MMC)

All the ground space within the ancient walls had long been filled but the graveyard was still used and the coffins had gradually been placed on top of the other, until they had risen to a height of ten feet above the surface. The coffins are not even covered with earth, but are only wrapped in turf. In some places they look like the steps of a stair covered with a carpet. One can count the tiers ... I was surprised that no foul smell pervaded this charnel pit, until the captain (MacDonald) pointed out that there were two holes made in the coffin by the rats, and that a body was no sooner left than it was devoured.

That description makes burial customs on St Colme sound like a modified continuance of the practice of corpse cleansing by eagles and seabirds that archaeologists recently discovered up in Orkney – a practice at least 5000 years old.

Traditional fairytales were still being told on St Kilda when my great-grandfather left. My daughter, Damaris, is going to present a selection of St Kildan stories with music and dance at the Edinburgh Festival. Most that we know tend to be short and sweet.

Once long ago, two men were passing a spot where a house now stands, but which was then a little green hill, when they heard a sound like butter being churned in an earthenware jar. One of the men cried out, 'Give us a drink, good wife,' and a door immediately opened, there in the hillock, and a strange woman came out and she presented a bowl of milk to the man who had asked for it. He declined to take it, so she handed it to the other man, who drank it down with great pleasure. She then disappeared back into the hillside, closing the door behind her. That same day, the man who had refused the milk fell over the cliff at Osimhal and was killed. The other lived a long and happy life – and told the story.

That's a wonderful little story – about sex and setting up home, I think! Another old story concerns the gift of bardic utterance. One day, a St Kildan woman was sitting alone in a hut, rocking her child in a cradle, when two strange women dressed in green entered the door and, by some magical power, deprived the mother of speech. She wanted to call out to her neighbours, but no sound came from her throat. One of the two women dressed in green then said, 'This child, I see, has drunk the milk of the cow that ate the "Mothan" and we can do nothing for him – but give him a great gift for language.' Well, that child was a wonderful talker and when he grew into a man he had the ability to compose a rhyme on any subject at the shortest notice. In fact this man was said to talk more than any six other men on the island. He was a bard! And it was his mother who first recognised his gift, which is not surprising! That bard was said to have died, on the island of Harris, at a time when grandfathers of men then living on St Kilda were still alive in 1875. Perhaps the St Kildans were glad to get rid of a man who talked six times more than their talkative selves!

When my father died we scattered his ashes by the standing stones on Machrie Moor, on the Isle of Arran. It was what he wanted. It was another place that he loved, and it's where Joujou's ashes will also be scattered.

When my daughter Damaris was born, her birth was the first video-recorded by the Southern General Hospital in Glasgow, and her birth became part of a television programme which won all kinds of prizes – in Sweden and Australia. Damaris says it won the prizes because her father was a priest and wore a kilt! I say it won because it captured the spirit of St Kilda –

Joujou Mitchell and Martine Chalmers, the Auvergne, 1997. (MMC)

Opposite.
St Kilda, Boreray and Stac Lee. (ERM)

boldness, survival, the heroic acceptance of the changeless wonder of life. No man is an island. No woman is an island. And there was something theatrical about life on St Kilda; there had to be.

Perhaps it was because the St Kildans lived such isolated lives that they developed this romantic and self-dramatising side to their natures. I've got it; my mother's got it; my grandfather Donald Ferguson had it; my daughter has it. And Martin Martin describes the St Kildans, of both sexes, as having 'a genius for poetry, and [they] compose entertaining verses and songs in their own language — which is very emphatical'. We're still emphatical and we're still romantic and I can still hear my grandfather Donald singing 'A Red, Red Rose'. There were never red roses on St Kilda, but in Paris Donald would bring great bunches for Mémé. My father grew red roses for Joujou in Bearsden, and Bernard grew them here in Kintyre, for me. Atlantic air is the best for roses.